flyfishing

THE
GREAT
WESTERN
RIVERS

flyfishing

THE GREAT WESTERN RIVERS

Written & photographed by RALPH KYLLOE

Gibbs Smith, Publisher
Salt Lake City

First Edition
08 07 06 05 04   5 4 3 2 1

Text and photographs © 2004 Ralph Kylloe

Published by
Gibbs Smith, Publisher
P.O. Box 667
Layton, Utah 84041

Orders: 1.800.748.5439
www.gibbs-smith.com

Cover design by Kurt Wahlner
Interior design by Lassiter Design: Maralee Lassiter
Printed in Hong Kong

Library of Congress Cataloging-in-Publication Data

Kylloe, Ralph R.
    Flyfishing the great western rivers / written and photographed by Ralph Kylloe—1st ed.
        p. cm.
    ISBN 1-58685-437-2
        1. Fly-fishing—West (U.S.)—Anecdotes. 2. Rivers—West (U.S.)—Anecdotes. 3. Kylloe, Ralph R. 1. Title.
SH464.W4 K95 2004
799.12'4'0978—dc22
                              2003027039

CONTENTS

For my father,
Ralph Kylloe, Sr.

ACKNOWLEDGMENTS

There are tons of people who helped with this book. I know I will forget some of them. It's not personal. It's just that as I get older I forget things that I should remember. This book has been in progress for several years and I am certain that I misplaced business cards of guides who helped or great B&Bs that put me up for a weekend.

Nonetheless, here goes: Many thanks to Doug and Janis Tedrow, Luke Connor, George Davis, Brian and Debbie Correll, Jack Melville, Barney and Susan Bellinger, Ed Link, Carlin Bennett, Ken Beatty, Keith Shorts, Chuck Paige, Bob and Liz Esperti, Kristie Piazzola, Harry Howard, Pam and Fred Rentschler, Bill Growning, Michael Henry, Mike and Steve Mauot, Bill McBurney, Dick Gil, Steve Ranney, Dave Salmon, Crazy John Jelinek, Greg Kupchak, Fred Telleen, Dan Dee, Dave Olsen, Dave Huber, Terry Ring, Chris Swersey, Dave Olsen, Jake Gaudet, Bill and Kitty Sperry, Pat Graham, Bill von Brendel, Heidi Weiskoph, Bob Siter, Charles Summerville, Andy Fisher, Kurt Kylloe and Tom Welsh. Special thanks to my wife Michele and to my daughter Lindsey. How they tolerate my passion for fishing I'll never know, but thank God they do!

A very special thank you to my friend and editor, Madge Baird. She was incredibly instrumental in pulling together hundreds of pages of notes written by myself over the years. This book would never have been completed without her guidance, organizational skills and ability to rein in my thoughts. How she tolerates me and makes sense of my ramblings, I'll never know. She is the queen of all editors. Thanks also to associate editor Hollie Keith and assistant editor Johanna Buchert Smith.

FOREWORD

Jack Dennis has often said that not even the world's greatest guide can control whether or not the trout are going to be biting. He's also stood firm in his belief that the discerning guide can always control more important things like the caliber of his or her company and food.

Ralph Kylloe is a discerning guide. Flooding the reader with fond memories while prompting dreams of trips yet to be, his photographs enrich each page with genuineness. Ralph's writing is real and alive, pithy and poignant. In tandem with his insightful photographs, it captures the essence of what it means to be a fisherman. Ralph's stories ring true as they entertain.

Fly-fishing and Kylloe go together like bread and butter.

Meet Dr. Kylloe, the consummate Renaissance man, artist, artisan, musician, businessman, merchant, poet and professor.

Meet Ralph, the kid eager for new adventures in learning and experiencing; a student of a man living life in big gulps while studying the little things simply for the joy of it.

Meet my friend Ralph, a middle-aged man-child of a fly fisherman who can't get enough of stronger knots, fourteen-foot-plus hand-tied leaders, double hauling, more colorful streamers, smaller midges, heavier nymphs, lighter boots and tighter lines.

This is not a book about technique or catching but rather a whimsical dalliance into the adventure of it all: a walk with a master storyteller painting every page with photographs and prose that speak "fisherman."

This Kylloe book captures the tone, the style, the grace, the reverence, and the wonderment implicit in the fly-fishing experience.

ROBERT A. ESPERTI
FORMER MEMBER, U.S. FLY FISHING TEAM

INTRODUCTION

I go through phases. I caught my first fish when I was about four years old. For many years I fished with a fly rod. Then I got hooked on bass fishing. For years, in the wintertime, I traveled to Florida to catch tons of huge bass in the wonderful lakes throughout the region. But all things change.

Several years ago my good friend Barney Bellinger told me to give him a thousand dollars. He said it was for new fishing gear. So I gave him the money. I didn't argue. I just gave him the money. The following morning he showed up with two new fly rods, reels, and all kinds of related gear. That was it.

And so I started fly-fishing. And like other activities I've gotten involved in, I jumped in with ardent fervor. I lived and breathed fly-fishing. In time, I began to write about my experiences. I showed many of the stories to my editors who have been responsible for my other books. They were encouraging. As a photographer, I also made photos of many of my trips. Many of the areas I have fished are stunning. Hopefully, the photos depict the beauty and ruggedness of the rivers that have captured the imagination of all fly fishermen.

This book is not only about the great western rivers but also about the rich experiences that surround the art of fly-fishing.

I know I'll receive tons of letters and e-mails berating me for not including this or that particular river. In truth, I couldn't include all the rivers I wanted to fish. There are so many wonderful rivers in the West that one could never fish all of them. But, for one reason or another, I found myself in the vicinity of the rivers included in this book. And people kept mentioning that I had to fish a certain river. "It's the greatest and the most beautiful," they would say. So I would hire a guide and fish the river they had suggested. I was never disappointed.

I've never been on a river I didn't like. Sometimes rivers are too crowded or I don't catch anything, but the truth is, I love fly-fishing and every river has some elements of beauty in it. I don't have a favorite river. Nonetheless, some are more beautiful than others: the Smith River in California or Lee's Ferry in Arizona or many others for that matter.

In truth, fly-fishing is a solitary activity. Sure, you can go with your friends and at the end of the day you can have a great time telling stories. But it's still a very personal, isolated experience. In my early years as a fisherman I used to watch fly fishermen standing alone in the middle of a river working on their tackle. I always wondered what they were doing.

January 30

THE JED SMITH RIVER

Fly-fishing is
a profound art.
Catching fish
only makes
it better.

In far northern California, the Smith River

meanders through the Jedediah Smith Redwoods State Park. Certainly one of my all-time favorite rivers, the scenery is complex and stunning. Lush in every way, the immediate environment clearly belongs to the druids and trolls of our imaginations. The redwood trees themselves are by far the most ethereal and dramatic of all the organic creations belonging to the earth. Soaring to the heavens, they are nothing less than stunning statements to the uniqueness and magic of life on this planet. And through all this wanders an absolutely gorgeous river that several species of salmon and trout call their home.

I had been traveling in the area with my wife, Michele, and daughter, Lindsey, and had spent a few days just walking in the woods, enjoying the scenery and making photos. The air was about thirty degrees. Although I had spoken with a few local guides, all of them told me to save my money since there were presently no fish in the river. I was advised to wait another two weeks, when the first major run of steelhead would be entering the river.

But I'm a die-hard optimist and finally convinced a guide to take me out the following morning. After arranging my trip, I wandered through the forest near the river, enjoying the majesty of the area.

At first I thought it might be a jumbo jet crashing. It was such a horrible sound — first low in tone, then growing tremendously louder to the point that I thought the earth was coming to an end. The ground both trembled and shook and my only thought was that I was in the middle of a monstrous West Coast earthquake. It was a sickening sensation. I learned not long after that a giant fifteen-hundred-year-old redwood had fallen just a few blocks from where I was walking. The tree had come down in the middle of the Smith River. It fell so violently and with such great weight that it knocked about a hundred acres of water out of the river. Eyewitnesses said they were shocked at the force of the tree falling and hitting the earth.

The following morning I entered the river in a classic drift boat. It was just about daybreak and the guide and I wore heavy winter jackets over our waders. Frost and steam were everywhere, like the breath of a sleeping giant on an icy day. At least three other boats with guides entered the water with us. I was happy to see that I was not the only "fishing fool" on the water.

We were fishing for early steelhead, but I suspect that the guide would have been happy with anything, including carp or catfish. It was an interesting way to fish. Large globs of gooey salmon eggs are fixed to a hook. A heavy, two-ounce weight is fixed eighteen inches above the hook. The entire mess is then cast upstream and allowed to bounce its way along the bottom through a set of rapids. A strike usually occurs on the swing of the run as the bait slows near the end of the rapids.

I got the hang of the process fairly quickly. It wasn't a pretty way to fish but what the heck; it was far better than spending the day watching TV. Besides, the scenery along the river was extraordinary. But it was also so cold that ice would form on the eyelets of the poles and had to be cleared away after every other cast.

We spent maybe a half hour around the first hole. My guide told me that it was only necessary to put a few salmon eggs on the hook. "Many times the steelhead will hit when just one egg is on the line," said the guide. We left the first set of rapids empty-handed, and we came up with nothing on the second and third set of rapids as well.

At the fourth set, I changed tactics. I fixed a huge glob of eggs to the hook and cast upstream. In cold water fish slow down. I figured that to get the fish to strike, the rewards would have to be significant, so why not use plenty of eggs? At first, the guide berated me for using so many eggs. "Don't waste them," he said. I held my rod high to take up any slack in the line and waited.

BAM! The strike indicator went down like a rocket. Moments later, the rod bent in half. Then, a twenty-eight-inch steelhead made three consecutive jumps near the boat. The guide couldn't believe it — we were both thrilled. I fought the fish for several minutes as it made three major runs away from the boat, taking at least thirty yards of line on each run. Soon it quieted and I was able to bring it near the boat. Once it was netted, an examination revealed several sea lice affixed to its body. As sea lice fall off quickly

[OPPOSITE] *Wandering through the Jed Smith Redwoods State Park, the Smith River is lined with towering redwood trees. The color of the water is often strikingly turquoise blue.*

The Smith River has impressive runs of salmon and steelhead. Michele Kylloe throws a dry fly to an eddy looking for an elusive trout.

once they arrive in freshwater, we knew this steelhead was fresh from the sea. I gently removed the small hook from his mouth, quietly thanked him for his efforts and released him back to the cool waters of the Smith River. He swam quietly and quickly from the boat.

The next set of rapids produced two more fish of equal size. And after each fish or each cast, I placed another big glob of fresh fish eggs on the hook. At the next set of rapids I had two major hits and fought each for several minutes before losing them. Then I landed a thirty-inch steelhead that we fought for a good half hour. When

a hooked fish is able to make it back into the rapids, it becomes much more difficult to land. On this occasion we had to follow the fish in the boat for quite some distance before it was no longer able to use the power of the water to escape from us. Finally on shore, I was able to turn him close to the net and bring him under control. Once he was in the net, the hook just dropped out with no effort from me. If I had let any slack in the line at all, the fish would have spit the hook in my face. I released him back to his home world. He was happy to be gone.

At the end of the day I had landed five great fish and lost two more. One of the fish hooked itself in the gills and we decided to keep it for dinner. My guide told me that I'd had the greatest day of steelhead fishing on the Smith River he had ever seen. That night at the hotel the chef prepared the fish dinner for Michele and me, and I insisted that he join us for dinner, which he did! Later I received five phone calls from other guides asking me if my fishing record was true. I was the talk of the entire town. Even the woman at the front desk commented that she had personally fished the Smith River for forty years and had never caught a steelhead! I went to sleep happy that night.

Wishing for an early start in the morning, we had a quick breakfast while it was still dark. Wanting to show Michele a bit of the river, we drove to the boat launch where I had put in the day before. There before us, we counted thirty-five boats, each waiting their turn to put into the water. Each boat had at least two fishermen and a guide. Each person, no doubt, had high hopes of catching as many fish as the guy from New York had caught the day before. Near the front of the line of people waiting, I saw the guide I had fished with the day earlier. He saw me as well, and gave me a huge grin and a thumbs-up sign! I wished him and the fishermen a quiet good luck and then drove off.

Later that night I called the hotel clerk where we had stayed the night before and asked how the fishing was. "Lotta boats in the water today," she said, "but no one caught a thing. Come back in a couple of weeks when the steelhead are in," she said. Sometimes we have to give thanks to the gods for gifts granted.

The following summer I was again in the Jed Smith State Forest gazing at the redwoods. The richness of the green flora was mesmerizing. The Smith River was low. The salmon and the steelhead had long gone to places I would never know. Only a few native trout remained. So what would I be if I didn't try? Out came my wading sandals, fishing vest, fly rod and flies. I wore only swim trunks and sandals as I wandered in. I ignored the crispness of the snowmelt water.

Trout don't like open water or sunshine. They like structure and shade. They like to hide and jump their prey at the last second. The water was deceptively clear as I found myself chest-deep only a few feet from shore. To get to the shady side of the river was impossible. I can cast nearly seventy-five feet accurately, but it was much farther to the shady shore. I caught few fish that day.

Most fishermen know that fishing is not always about catching fish. But to stand in the clear Smith River, surrounded by towering redwoods, basking in the sun and blue sky, throwing flies was the reward. Picking up floating line from the water, pulling it behind you and propelling it to a perfect spot in front of you is the reward. The dance of the floating line as it glides gracefully through the air, controlled completely and artfully by the fisherman, is no different than a ballerina's glide across a stage. Great art brings great pleasure.

Fly-fishing is a profound art. Serious fly fishermen know this. Catching fish only makes it better. Fishing with flies is an activity that gracefully matures through the years. The more I do it, the more proficient I become, and the more I enjoy it. It makes my life better. ⌒

May 30

OREGON

FRESHWATER

I am

embarrassed

to say that

I lost my

first eleven

strikes.

We had driven south from Portland, Oregon,

toward the town of Elkton, about halfway down the state. The wonderful folks at the Big K Lodge had invited us to spend a few days fishing with them, even though the lodge would be officially closed while we were there, hosting an all-night graduation party for the town's high school graduates.

[THIS PAGE] *Midsummer brings calm, slow waters on the Rogue. Huge rainbows and an occasional summer run of steelhead often school up in deep holes where the water is cooler and food more plentiful.*

[THIS PAGE] *Rocky shores and rushing rapids sometimes discourage fishermen from trying their luck. Seen here in midsummer, the Rogue seems inviting. In the spring the water level dramatically rises and prevents any access to the river.*

We had trouble finding the entrance to the Big K — actually passed it twice. We didn't mind the drive though, as the view along the Umpqua is quite spectacular and we stopped at several good-looking fishing holes to test the waters, catching fish on just about every cast. We made our way to the small town of Sutherlin, where we had an extraordinary Mexican dinner at La Pedro's.

Later that evening we arrived at the Big K, located off a dirt road more than four miles long. The entire facility is almost brand new, and the log complex boasts numerous clean, modern log cabins, a large dining hall and meeting facilities large enough to keep several hundred people happy.

The grounds were impressive. The Big K encompasses 2,500 acres of pristine land. In the

[THIS PAGE]   *The drive into the Big K Ranch is a visual feast. Passing ancient farms and green fields, the Umpqua River flows peacefully through the countryside of Oregon.*

immediate backyard are several hundred cows and sheep. A pond with monster trout welcomes any angler willing to test their skills. Eagles and osprey soar just out of reach.

But I liked the river most of all: crystal clear and as natural as could be. I could see fish rising as the sun sank beyond the lush green mountains. Inviting as it was, I would wait until the morning to try my luck.

The evening drew to a close as I walked with my wife and daughter near the banks of the river and in the pasture. We ran into the senior owner of the lodge, Sam Kesterson, who charmed us with local stories. While we chatted, Lindsey tried to feed the sheep, but they liked their privacy and avoided contact with us, so we took to catching grasshoppers and feeding them to the trout in the pond. It was a grand evening. We soon retired to our cabin as a bus full of the graduating teenagers arrived at the lodge.

It was surprising how quiet they were. As an insomniac, I am up at all hours of the night. I checked in on them at two, three and then at five in the morning. The party was going strong all night! But there were only twelve graduates plus friends and a few parents, so the party never really had a chance to get rowdy.

The following morning we enjoyed a great breakfast cooked by the owners of the lodge. When we met our guide, I asked him about fishing for trout in the river below. "There are no trout in the river," he said. "It's too hot for them." With that said, I really didn't know what was in store for us. I was mystified and even a bit disappointed, but open to any type of adventure. In retrospect, I hadn't the slightest need to be disappointed.

The nice thing about owning such a large portion of land directly along the river is that guides can stay right on company property and not have to worry about parking places, tickets or other concerns. We put in just a mile or so above the lodge and hopped into a drift boat with our fly rods and other necessary gear.

[THIS PAGE] *This classic fat Rogue River rainbow was taken on a dry fly and successfully released back to its home waters.*

[OPPOSITE] *The Rogue River offers not only quiet solitude but violent rapids as well. Here fly fishermen cast for rainbows and smallmouth bass.*

We were fishing for shad, a popular game fish. The method for catching these characters is similar to back trolling. I was surprised at how much finesse it took and am embarrassed to say that

I lost my first eleven strikes. My wife, on the other hand, caught her first five fish and lost no opportunity to remind me of her prowess and deft hand with a fly rod.

But soon I got the hang of it and managed to start hooking the little beasts with the best of them. Shad were the surprise fish of the year for me. Good-looking little critters, they fought like gangbusters. They seemed to school up, and once a pocket of them was found, it was one right after the other. There was no waiting and no rest for the wicked. Ranging from one to three pounds, they are a worthy game fish that should not be overlooked or underrated. We had more fun that morning than I thought we would.

But the day only got better and more interesting. After lunch the guide suggested that we try smallmouth bass. Fine with me, I thought.

The highest form of the art of fly-fishing includes the use of dry flies. Floating a fly on the surface, the strikes are a marvel to watch. Our guide suggested the use of Chernobyl ants. Perhaps the strangest and most stupid looking of all the flies created by humans, Chernobyl ants are made from a thin piece of foam and enhanced with small legs made of rubber. They come in all sizes and colors and I can only assume that they were made to resemble a salmon fly hatch or something like that. At any rate, I had used them with great success in Wyoming, so why not give them a try here?

On they went. Tied to four-pound tippet material, they resembled water gliders as we landed them gently on the river's surface. With my first cast, a massive boiling swirl engulfed my fly. A beautiful smallmouth came to my waiting hands for a ride. Every cast resulted in a hit. The clear water added greatly to the fun as the fish could be seen as soon as they began their attack. And it wasn't just one fish. As we would reel the fish to the boat, we could see many other fish attacking the one on the line.

To add to the fun, I placed a small drop nymph on the Chernobyl ant and cast it to the shore. Bam! I had my first double of the day! A fish each on both the ant and the nymph! When I lost a fish on either of the flies, another fish would attack and be caught by the time I got the flies back in the boat! This was truly fishing at its finest.

Throughout the day the guide told us stories of the region and of fishing on the impressive Umpqua River. After a full eight hours of fishing, we were nearly exhausted from reeling in line; I fully doubt that there was ever more than a five-minute break between fish on either Michele's or my line. The fish weren't huge – no larger than three pounds – but the action was extraordinary.

That evening we had dinner and ice cream at a rustic old restaurant in Elkton, and the following morning we were off for another adventure. I can only say the Big K is one of the finest and friendliest fishing lodges we have ever had the pleasure visiting. I look forward to our next visit.

As we left the area we stopped at several picturesque sites along the river and cast, with great success, any number of different flies to waiting smallmouths. I could have stayed in the area for a month and been quite happy.

[THIS PAGE-ABOVE] *The Deschutes River, flowing through northern Oregon and into the Columbia River, passes through stark, arid countryside populated by deer and rattlesnakes, requiring one to watch where they are walking.*

[THIS PAGE-RIGHT] *Like most rivers, the Deschutes is complete with numerous put-ins that allow for easy access to the water.*

[OPPOSITE] *Michele Kylloe shows off a pair of smallmouth bass taken with a fly rod on the Umpqua. The bass struck a hopper on top as well as a bead-head nymph as a dropper hung below the primary dry fly.*

[ABOVE] *Dramatic rapids are a main feature of the Deschutes. The piers are stands from which Native Americans use traditional methods to capture salmon.*

[ABOVE] Casting a line into the Deschutes. In an effort to retain the quality of the fishery, fisher-men are not allowed to fish from boats. In recent years the river has undergone dramatic changes due, in part, to the excessive use of water for agriculture purposes.

[LEFT] Deschutes rainbows are called "red sides" because of their dramatic red stripes.

June 10

ADVENTURES IN ALASKA

Fishing is the
ultimate expression
of optimism—
on every cast is
the possibility of
catching the world's
largest fish.

On a trip to Alaska one time,

I spent the night in Seattle before I caught my plane north. As I arrived at the airport terminal I noticed a large, black, stretch limousine pull abruptly to the curb. Four Japanese men in dark suits got out, stood in line to get their tickets, went through security and waited patiently to board the plane. They were serious men of expensive taste. Their luggage included leather-cased fishing poles, laptop computers and camera bags. Two aids, who were obviously subordinate to the other four, showed up and appeared to take charge of the carry-on luggage.

We all boarded the plane and took our seats; I was two rows in front of them. I could not help but notice that they made frequent demands on the flight attendants. They seemed less than polite.

Everyone settled in; I read several magazines and dreamed of huge trout and the mighty rivers of Alaska. Near the middle of the flight I rose and went to the rear of the plane to use the restroom. As I returned, the four Japanese men were closely huddled over a laptop computer. As I passed them, to my horror and shock, the plane took a violent lunge downward. I threw out my hands to catch myself and unfortunately slammed my hand directly on the keypad of the laptop. Within seconds, the laptop went haywire and started flashing lights and displaying a bizarre mix of numbers.

[18]

With that, one of the Japanese men hit the ceiling. He started screaming at me. Apparently I had ruined his program and all his memory. He broke into a long shouting speech in Japanese, very irritated and red in the face. Shockingly, he had to be physically restrained by his three cohorts. They actually had to hold the guy down for a good minute until he calmed down. In the meantime, I just stood there trying to explain in English that all this was a complete accident, apologizing to them several times for the incident. Even the flight attendants got involved in trying to calm everyone down. This strange scene went on for ten minutes.

After everyone returned to their seats, I could hear the four men frantically and diligently working on the computer to get the thing operating again. Frankly, I don't think they ever succeeded.

The plane landed shortly and I got off and wandered down to the baggage claim to retrieve my gear. Once in the baggage area, one of the men came up to me. "Dr. Kylloe san," he began, after bowing deeply to me. I returned his bow. "I want to apologize for the behavior of our colleague. He acted inappropriately. He is a hot hair." I chuckled and corrected him saying that the term is *hot head!* I could not figure out how he knew my name.

"I hope that you accept this small gift as a token of our sincerity." He handed me a leather case that no doubt contained a fishing rod.

"I cannot accept this. It was an accident. Please apologize to your colleague again for me."

[OPPOSITE] *Tom Welsh from New York battles a large rainbow on the Kenai in the fall.*
[THIS PAGE] *Greg Kupchak fights a salmon on the upper section of the Kenai.*

"Please, Dr. Kylloe, accept the gift. We would be dishonored if you did not." He was dead serious.

I took the pole. He bowed deeply and disappeared. I never saw him or his party again.

That night in my hotel room I opened the case. It contained a stunningly beautiful ten-foot fly rod. It handled magnificently. The wood on the handle was highly figured and the rod was hand inscribed with perfect Japanese characters. The guides were meticulously and flawlessly wrapped and the color of the rod was unlike anything I had ever seen. It was a superb piece of artwork.

I used the pole only once during that trip to Alaska. I cast with it only a few times and then returned it to its case. It was clearly far more valuable than I had originally thought.

Three weeks later, while I was in a tackle shop paying the guide for his day's efforts, someone broke into my rental car and stole the pole, all my fishing gear, including two other expensive rods, all my cameras and three weeks' worth of photographs containing hundreds of pictures of bears and fish I had caught during my stay. To this day, my heart sinks to my stomach when I think of it.

JUNE 10   The flight was to be at five in the evening. At 3:30, I said good-bye to Michele and Lindsey at the airport and checked in. Due to storms in Chicago, the flight was delayed from taking off for a half hour. After boarding, it was delayed another hour and a half as we sat on the ground. I was relieved when we finally took off. Once we were near Chicago, we were put in a holding pattern and finally sent to Detroit for refueling. I knew I was going to miss my flight to Alaska. We finally landed in Chicago at 1:30 a.m. I stood in line for more than an hour to reschedule my flight. Unfortunately, they closed the service desk just before it was my turn at the counter. I would have to wait until 6 a.m. to reschedule. I was invited to sleep on a cot in the basement of O'Hare until the airport was reopened. The basement was like a refugee camp; more than 500 people were on cots in varying stages of sleep.

The guards woke us at 4 a.m., after only an hour's nap. I stood in line for another hour and was told that I would have to take a flight later that day to San Francisco and then another flight to Anchorage that evening. I took the tickets.

After another hour of waiting, I approached a different ticket counter and fortunately got the last seat on a direct flight to Anchorage that was leaving shortly. I was thrilled. But seven hours on an airplane really is no fun. I was also acutely aware that my luggage, including fishing poles and tackle, would no doubt be lost in the shuffle. But surprise of surprises, once I finally arrived in Alaska, I was relieved to find all my luggage and fishing gear safe. The car rental also went smoothly, a sign that the bad luck of the last thirty hours might be ending. I was happily in Alaska and looking forward to a month of rainbow trout, sockeyes, kings and stunning scenery!

A fisherman with a nice sockeye salmon. Whenever a fish was on the line, the dog lunged into the water and retrieved the catch.

Later that evening, I checked into a small but comfortable cabin at Gwin's Lodge in the rustic Alaskan town of Cooper Landing, about two hours south of Anchorage. Resting on the wilds of the extraordinary Kenai River, the only reason Cooper Landing exists at all is for fishing. After I unpacked my bags, I wandered over to the restaurant at Gwin's and had a great fresh halibut sandwich, after which I passed out, fully dressed, in my cabin.

Alaska is a funny place during the summer. Twenty-four-hour daylight messes with you. I could not sleep. At midnight it's plenty light enough out to read and people are actually out doing stuff. So at 2 a.m. I bought a fishing license and went fishing with my spinning rod for sockeye about two minutes from my cabin. By 2:30 I was back at my cabin, having caught my limit on three consecutive casts! I finally went to sleep and woke at eight in the morning.

The sockeye (also called reds) salmon run on the Kenai River defies comprehension. Beginning in June, more than 100,000 sockeye enter the Kenai River and make their way to the backwaters of the river solely for the purpose of reproducing. Averaging seven to ten pounds and a little more than three feet long, they come close to being the perfect fish. Heavily regulated and closely watched, fishermen are allowed to take as many as three a day. Catch and release as many as you want, but three is the limit.

So at nine in the morning I drove to the Russian River Ferry, just a few miles from Gwin's, paid the parking and ferry fee and ventured into the almost unbelievable land of the sockeye fisherman. Separated by about ten feet on either side of each other were perhaps a thousand fishermen lined up neatly on the banks of the Upper Kenai River. Combat fishing at its finest!

At face value, most people who come to Alaska really do want a wilderness experience. Most want no other people, no TVs, computers, cell phones, stock market quotes, noise, crime or other vestiges of modern society. Many people want nothing to do with the crowds or combat fishing. But in truth, combat fishing isn't all that bad. It's cheap, which, for many, is a major consideration — the cost of parking and a ferry ride is all it takes. Almost all of the fishermen are incredibly polite and friendly. Most will be very helpful. And the fishing is absolutely great. You can catch your limit in just a few minutes if you can get the technique down.

Most of my first full day of fly-fishing (combat fishing with a fly rod is not really fly-fishing) on the river, I caught nothing. I lost a dozen flies, broke my line many times and was disappointed. I felt like a fool. I looked great in my high-end waders, new vest and expensive gear, but I didn't catch a thing. Actually, I was downright miserable.

Combat fishing is a sport for those who don't mind fishing elbow-to-elbow.

Just when I was about to leave, a new guy showed up and coached me through the experience. I needed better flies and a full one-ounce sinker. The fish were on the bottom and the expression "If you're not on the bottom, you're not fishing" was the truism of the day. My neighbor gave me six flies and equally as many weights. He also showed me a new knot and how to position the gear on my fly rod. He spent time showing me how to do a backhand flip with the line and how far out the fly should be. The entire process was very different from fishing with dry flies on the rivers near my home in the Adirondacks.

From that time on, I caught fish, one right after the other. My neighbor refused to take money for the gear he had given me. Believe me when I say that I really appreciated his efforts to guide me through the routine. As I have suggested many times before, when you go fishing in a new lake or area, it pays to hire a guide to show you how to fish and where the fish are. You can waste tons of time and money or you can hire a guide and learn the ropes in a short period. The choice is yours.

But there are other things about combat fishing that are unique, as well. You can get into the motion of the experience. I call it the dance of the river (or, please excuse me, river dance). Fishermen become synchronized in their movements. A backhand flip cast requires that you have the rod and reel in your right hand. The current is going downstream. Everyone, at just about the same time, flips their line upstream. Because people are standing so close to each other, it's a necessity that everyone do this at the same time. If not, lines by the millions would become tangled. On several occasions, I watched with amazement as hundreds of people were in just about perfect synchronization! And this only ceases when someone shouts, "FISH ON!" This, of course, causes a sudden lapse in the dance, but fish are why we're all here in the first place. Once the fish is landed, the entire dance resumes.

It's not a perfect system but with many people, there is very little alternative. Throughout the day problems can occur. Unfortunately, once in a while some people can have a few too many beers and get LOUD, lines do become tangled, and occasionally someone comes and stands just a few feet from you and hogs your space. Often, inexperienced fishermen will try to join in and seem to tangle everyone's line. But all in all, when the fish are biting, all this is overlooked and people settle in to enjoy the day. Really, I have no objection to combat fishing. If you don't like it, don't do it. On the other hand, and I say this only after I have fished with a large number of other fishermen for a while, sometimes enough is enough.

My one low point occurred when a new fisherman appeared right next to me — I mean, we were touching shoulders. I had caught several fish from my point of ground and he wanted part of the action. On his first three casts he tangled me each time. It was not a casual mess but one that took several minutes to untangle. On his fourth cast he again created a mess of a "bird's nest" out of my line and his. In irritation, I took out a knife, cut his line and threw it in the water. He got the message and left my area.

The Setting

So I fished the Kenai for the first two days I was there. It was great fun. I met all kinds of people. The most frequently asked question was, "Where are you from?" For a while, I fished with a group from Germany and then another group from Japan. Both groups were well dressed and had top-notch equipment. No one in the groups spoke any English whatsoever. I made many photos of these people catching fish and was given business cards and asked for copies of the photos. I was invited for lunch with the Japanese. On the spot, they filleted one of the salmon and we had the freshest sushi lunches ever. They even provided sake for the occasion.

The Germans brought along their own chef. He built a small fire, laid out a portable table and chairs and cooked sausage for the men. I wasn't invited, so I sat by myself and ate my bologna sandwich. I caught more fish than they did. Every time I caught one, I could hear them talking. I think they were envious. You have to love it!

THE ZONE

Fishing is exactly like many other human endeavors. For some, it becomes a passion; for others, just a way to pass the time. It can become a significant art form. The most interesting thing about fishing is that it is, I believe, the ultimate statement of optimism. On every cast is the possibility of catching the world's largest fish. Each fisherman truly believes this. There is also the quest for the unknown. Beneath the water is a world so foreign to us that it lies beyond comprehension. You never know what to expect. You never know what will hit your line or what you will drag from the bottom. It is that realm of the unknown that mystifies us.

Water is also, ultimately, from where we all came. The rhythmic sounds of pounding waves speak deeply to us. We seek both serenity and comfort at the water's edge. It is a place for introspective moments and quiet solitude. It is a place where we go to mourn our losses and to rejuvenate our souls. It is a place to contemplate the great questions in our lives. The catching of fish, for many, is actually a very small part of the spiritual act of standing by the water's edge and the art of fishing. There is a lot more to it than the catching of fish.

But there are other things as well. When a fish is on the line, nothing else exists in the world. Time does not exist. It actually freezes. No other thoughts enter the mind. We enter "the zone." Nothing else matters. We become complete within ourselves; all our thoughts are concentrated and everything else is blocked out. Nothing else exists. And is it fun!

This concept is common in philosophical and psychological literature today. Psychologists often refer to this phenomenon as a "peak experience" or "flow." Those who have studied sociological patterns also refer to this as a "leisure" experience. A leisure experience is actually a state of mind that comes about as a result of a recreational experience. It can be achieved through a passionate interest and involvement in some form of activity. ■

Alaskan locals are fun, as well. I like people who are unique in character. Many of those I photographed were picturesque in their free-spirit outfits and beards down to their knees. Down-home Alaskans don't really care much for fancy outfits from high-end stores. They buy their gear from Wal-Mart, yard sales and second-hand stores. They catch just as many fish as, if not more than, the fancy dressers. They drive rusted old pickup trucks or RVs, and look and act the part of true Alaskans.

One elderly gentleman sat in the "handicapped only" section and caught more fish per hour than anyone else I watched on the river. "Ya gotta spit a big hocker on the bait if you want to catch fish," he said to me. I loved the guy. I watched him for a long time. He was paralyzed in his legs and had very little strength or movement in his arms. He actually had an aid cast his line. He then used a small remote electric winder to retrieve his line. He was very good at it. I wondered if I would have the luck that he had. I greatly admired his attitude.

Later that evening, I watched him struggle out of his wheelchair and into a beat-up van. I helped him into his vehicle, which was full of old newspapers, beer cans, cigarette butts and tires. "Thanks, bubba," he said to me. I never saw him again. I wish I had. Encounters with characters enrich one's life. Until we realize this, we cannot consider ourselves mature individuals. We have no time to lose.

The First Fly-In

It was Thursday and the owner of Gwin's, Bob Siter, insisted that I go on this trip. "You won't be disappointed," he said. With that in mind, I whipped out my trusty charge card and signed on the dotted line.

At 6:30 in the morning, I pulled into the parking lot of Talon Air Service, just outside of Soldotna, Alaska. I was greeted by a number of people and within a half hour was on a 1956 Beaver pontoon heading across Cook Inlet. We flew in a heavy fog and could see the mountains before us but not the land below. My blood pressure kept rising as the mountains got closer and closer — and I really do mean close. Suddenly, I was jolted to my seat as we descended quickly into the fog. Without warning, we took another serious jolt and the pilot landed our plane on calm water. After a forty-five-minute flight, we had landed on Wolverine Lake.

[OPPOSITE] *In the shadow of Redoubt Volcano, on the east side of Cook Inlet, flows the Wolverine River. The river is a haven for sightseers, bear watchers and fly fishermen taking advantage of a huge yearly run of sockeye salmon.* [THIS PAGE] *The entryway to many of the wilderness rivers in Alaska is through the doors of a 1950s DeHavilland Beaver. Most bush pilots in Alaska fly these antique planes because of their durability.*

We transferred to a motored rowboat that was tied up on the shore and shortly were whipping along at full throttle in a dense fog on Wolverine Creek. Soon the boat slowed and we docked on the shore. The entire setting was beautiful: the water was perfectly calm, the snowcapped mountains in the distance were stunning and huge sockeye salmon were rising second by second! Now, if they would just hit my flies, I would be happy.

It didn't take long to find out. One right after the other, they slammed into our lines. I caught my limit in ten minutes.

Soon another boat showed up. Then several more pontoons landed with more people. There were a good hundred fishermen on the banks. Everyone caught fish. Next to me were a gentleman with two young kids and his wife. His kids were bored and his wife tried fishing but lacked the passion to continually throw a line into the water.

So every time I got a fish on my line, I would call the young boy over and let him fight the fish. Once he caught one, I would let the young girl catch one. Between the two kids, they probably fought ten to fifteen ten-pound salmon. The kids were having a great time, but I noticed that whenever the father got a fish on the line, he chose to fight it himself. In the back of my mind I hoped that he would share the experience with his kids. I hoped that he spent time with them. Kids need that sort of stuff.

After lunch we departed for another part of the water system. After a twenty-minute boat ride, we wound up near a falls where there were supposed to be bears. Unfortunately, the salmon had not traveled that far upriver and the bears were nowhere in sight. We ended the day with the catching of a few more fish and then left toward home on the vintage airplane. The trip back was far more eventful (in a positive way) than the trip out. I weaseled my way into the copilot's seat and enjoyed the stunning scenery. On the flats area, we saw at least ten bears and their cubs fishing in low-lying streams. The pilot flew the plane about fifty feet above the ground so we could get a good look at them. It was a day filled with fun and excitement. I took my salmon to the smokehouse and enjoyed fresh smoked salmon for many days.

The Russian River

JUNE 15   The opening of the Russian River for sockeye is unlike anything I have ever seen. The Russian joins the Kenai River in the town of Cooper Landing. At midnight on June 15, people are allowed to enter the river and fish. Attendance at this event is like the Second Coming — I'm not kidding. This is a revered experience and not to be missed by those who cherish rituals.

I was ready. I had my flies and had tested my gear and techniques for

three days on the Kenai. At 10 p.m. on June 14, I got in line with hundreds of other cars full of fishermen. One by one, each vehicle stopped at the guardhouse and paid three dollars for the privilege to park. Unbeknownst to me was that many people had reserved their spaces years in advance and were allowed to pull into their reserved spots before everyone else. To my dismay, by the time it was my turn at the guardhouse, the park was closed and I had to leave my vehicle in an outer lot. No big deal, I thought to myself. I'll just walk. So I picked up my gear and camera bag and started walking. Little did I realize that it was three miles back to the river. It was also midnight and I was tired. After walking uphill for half an hour, I stuck out my thumb and got a ride in the back of a pickup truck.

Finally, I got to the river, but I could not find the stairs leading down the mountain to water. I started down the side of a cliff but fell and nearly broke my leg. After about a half hour of descending with my gear, I came to the "waters of promise."

At twenty yards across and not more than three feet deep, the Russian is not a big river. It's class-two water all the way. It was now 1 a.m. and the fishing was in full swing. Fishermen were standing ten feet apart on both banks and in the river as well. It was like New York's George Washington Bridge at 5 p.m. I finally found a spot and caught my limit of three fish within fifteen minutes. I fished for another hour, releasing what I caught. Around 2 a.m., I started back. Having asked for directions, I found the stairs leading up the mountain with little effort.

A sockeye salmon slams a fly on the Russian River.

But realities came to bear. My gear was heavy and I had thirty more pounds of fish with me. And I was just about four miles from my vehicle and no one, I mean no one, was on the road. This was in serious bear country. It was nearly 3 a.m. I smelled like fish. I was carrying three fresh fish in my bag. Suddenly, I heard a crashing of brush just twenty yards in front of me. I stopped dead. I was scared to death. Out jumped a monstrous dark brown animal that I could barely make out. This is it, I thought. I'm going to be killed by a bear. It turned out to be a moose (also dangerous but not attracted to fish). I turned around and resolved not to walk farther. I would sleep in the parking lot if necessary. I soon realized that, unfortunately, bears were everywhere.

Fortunately, after a half hour of indecision, I got a ride with the last truck going out for the night. I was very happy to finally get to my vehicle.

I fished the Russian on and off for the next week and I caught my limit each time. It is a picturesque setting not to be missed by those who don't mind the crowds. The fishing is extraordinary and the setting is magical.

The Refuge

After my night (in Alaska it's only *called* night; it's really daytime all the time — at least in June) on the Russian I got back to my room at about 3 a.m. and passed out in my waders. An hour later, the alarm went off. I was to meet fishing guide extraordinaire Fred Telleen of Mystic Waters Guide Service at 5 a.m. I had fished with Fred many times the previous year. As far as I am concerned, he's one of the best. When he says I should fish with him on a certain day, I will not, barring nuclear holocaust, miss the trip.

Guide Fred Telleen shows off a huge Alaskan trout.

So at 5 a.m. we met at Gwin's and were off on another adventure. "No time for breakfast," he said, "Let's go fishing."

Many of the rivers in Alaska are tightly controlled and regulated. This is done to ensure that the river and the fish population stay healthy. A section of the Kenai had been closed to fishing and was to reopen June 15. At 6 a.m. on the fifteenth, Fred, Gordon Enk and I put in on the Kenai at a section known as the Refuge.

This was to be a traditional day of fly-fishing for rainbow trout. Generally, fishing for rainbow on the Kenai is done in September because rainbows spend their time in Skilak Lake, below the upper section of the Kenai, and enter the river at the end of the salmon run in the fall to feed off the eggs and carcasses of dead salmon. Traditionally, trout fishing is very slow in the summer and it's almost a waste of time and money to try for them during the warm months.

I thought Fred might be "misguided" with his suggestion to trout fish on this particular day in June. However, there are several nice things about fishing in the fall as well. One is that the hordes of people are gone. The colors are also in full bloom and the moose rut is on, making the big bulls more visible. But I mostly like it because the people are gone.

There is one thing I learned about twenty years ago from fishing guide Harry McDonald, who fishes out of Campbell River on Vancouver Island. I was fishing for king salmon and Harry was the guide. We had caught nothing for four hours. I suggested that we might want to try different bait. Harry stuck his face inches from mine and assertively said, "Always do what the guide says!" To this day, I never disagree with a guide and I always catch fish. So off we went. Eagles were everywhere. The sun was shining. The water was clear.

This may seem strange and unprofessional to many fly fishermen out there, but I have learned that the following method is good for big fish, especially when fishing very fast water with an abundance of structure. Onto my fly line I tie, with a nail knot, a three-foot section of forty-pound test nylon line. Onto that, connected with a blood knot, goes about six feet of twenty-pound test line. A fly is tied directly onto that line. It's simple, strong and effective. No need to get fancy.

So, on this day I chose a black egg-sucking leech and put two small split shots about eighteen inches above the fly. Up against a shore on a gravel bed, I had my first strike. I landed a beautiful twenty-two-inch rainbow. Kenai rainbows, especially pre-spawn rainbows, are often very dark in color and this one was a beauty. I would have been happy to end the day with just that one fish. Then Gordon caught two about the same size. Please understand that any trout above twenty inches is highly prized and many serious fishermen go a lifetime without catching one that large. This is especially true for fishermen in the lower forty-eight who do not have access to high-quality fisheries.

Then we fished a seam just downstream of a drop-off. Gordon's first cast produced a twenty-six-inch trout. Then I caught a twenty-eight-inch rainbow, and then another huge one. Gordon landed another huge fish — bigger than any I caught. This was fine fishing!

Gordon's style was different from mine. He was using a ten-foot pole strung with light line. He could throw the fly a great distance beautifully. I was using a nine-foot pole with heavy line and sinkers. He masterfully played each fish. I have a tendency to hook a fish and bring it in as soon as possible, especially in fast-moving waters. I can do this because of my heavier gear and the fact that sometimes the longer the fish is in the water, especially in a fast current, the greater the likelihood of losing it. On average, it took us about ten minutes, and sometimes longer, to land each fish.

Large fish fight differently than small fish. Rainbow trout are known as jumpers and dancers. Many times they will jump out of the water five times. The large rainbows we were catching jumped very little. They just went down to the bottom and stayed down. Once in a while they would jump, but these were heavy fish and if we had tried to "horse" them, we would have lost them.

There were a few lulls during the day, but in general the fishing stayed strong. We welcomed an afternoon breeze, as the sun was hot and the water perfectly calm. That day, the smallest fish we caught was probably eighteen inches, the largest about thirty-two. These were fat, football-sized rainbow trout with a tendency toward dark color. They were each a marvel of creation, perfectly formed and stunningly beautiful. We landed eighteen trout that day and broke off a dozen more. I will never forget it. An occasional day like this melts away the drudgery and toil and headaches that many of us face in the world today. Thank God for rainbow trout! And thank you, Fred!

As all fishermen know, the activity of fishing allows us the pleasure of undisturbed thinking, ruminating, if you will. That evening, as I sat alone in the motel room, I contemplated the fact that I am getting older. Sometimes it scares me. I had noticed changes in my physical abilities as well as my mental approach to things. Life was speeding up — and I was slowing down.

[THIS PAGE] *Handling a large rainbow taken on the Kenai.*

At fifty-five years of age, I realized that most of my life was behind me. I had completed several things that had been my life goals as a young man. I had written many books, own two beautiful houses and a great art gallery, had become a competent musician and had played music with heroes of my younger days, and I have a beautiful wife and daughter.

Even so, my emotional baggage was still with me. One would have thought the emotional garbage that had hampered me as a younger man would be gone by the time I had reached senior citizenship. It is still around and probably never will leave. But that's what makes me my own person. Unique, with my own abilities and motivations, my hang-ups have helped to define my character and direct my life. I find I work best alone and when I am working for myself. Some things never change. I don't consider myself a profound person with great social skills. Nonetheless, I have found my place in the world. It's not exactly what I wanted when I was twenty, but I am reasonably happy.

As I look in the mirror I realize that I'm no longer the eighteen-year-old kid I once was. I often wish I could go back and undo the stupid things I did back then. I wish I could take back the dumb things I said to others. If I could, my life would be better, I often say to myself. I hope I have never hurt anyone or taken away their dignity. But these are the wishes of all men. We can't undo what we have done earlier in our lives. We can only hope to do better with the time we have left.

I now struggle with my future goals. What are my dreams for the future? What else do I want out of life? What challenges will make me a better person? How much time do I have left?

Life is just a blur now. There is nothing I can do to slow it down. I am only buying memories — things I can write about and think about in the future. It's as if the present does not exist. I do things only for the memory of them.

Ultimately, we all struggle with self-respect. In the end it's all any of us have. The way to self-respect is by meeting the trials and tribulations that are placed in front of us as best we can. Half-hearted attempts and quick solutions do not lead to honor and dignity. Mediocrity is the curse of the devil. It strips us of our dignity. Hence, the absolute importance to live one's life as a responsible being. It's necessary to continually cultivate oneself by constantly learning new things and acquiring new skills. It's vital to find wonder and beauty in things and people. It's necessary to treat people right. It's necessary to do the things you are supposed to do, to pay attention to details. That's where we find the art and beauty in life. There is no time to lose.

[THIS PAGE] *A large rainbow taken on a Russian River salmon fly.*

Back to the Russian

JUNE 17   The alarm went off at 2 a.m. I had slept for only an hour. It was just about bright daylight out. I cleaned myself up, got dressed and jumped into the rental car. I saw two moose as I drove the five minutes toward the meeting place. I was still in Cooper Landing and was to meet Bob Siter, the owner of Gwin's, at 3 a.m. for some morning fishing on the Russian. Bob was bringing with him two of his employees who had never fished before. Both Brendan and Heather had worked all night and were excited about fishing.

By 3:15 we were unloading the truck and descending the stairs toward the Russian. A heavy fog was in the air and it was just a bit cooler than on the past several mornings. At the river, we became aware that the crowds of the weekend had dramatically thinned out. We followed Bob several hundred yards to his favorite fishing hole and entered the water.

First cast and "Fish on!" I kept the fish. The limit is three in possession. With my second cast I landed a beautiful silvery sockeye salmon. The water was only about three feet deep where we were standing. Bob landed several of his fish and spent time coaching Brendan through the finer points of flipping for salmon with a fly rod. Heather, who was standing behind me on the shore, had no waders and no pole, so whenever I hooked a fish, which was on just about every cast, I handed the pole to her to "play the fish in." She couldn't believe how much fun it was. That afternoon she purchased her own pole and hounded everyone to take her fishing. I can assure you that she had many accommodating offers.

Shortly, a number of other fishermen wandered into our area and mentioned that a moose and her twins had chased them off their spot just thirty yards upstream. We couldn't help but check out the moose for just a few minutes.

Fishing was almost ridiculous. For ten straight casts I had a fish on each one. After I had caught my limit, I removed the barb from my hook and caught and released another twenty or so. In time, I set down my pole and concentrated on making photos.

By 6 a.m. we had caught so many fish that we felt guilty. After cleaning the few we kept, we headed back to the truck and then back to Gwin's for a lo-cal breakfast of one pancake, orange juice and water. If I had eaten myself into oblivion with more food, I might have slept the rest of the day. But with the fish biting, there was no way I was going to let that happen. I did stop by my room, however, for a short nap!

The Kenai River can be both calm and aggressive. Gathering clouds are indicative of the almost daily storms that occur in the region.

Gaining the Kenai

JUNE 18   It's about 2:30 a.m. and I'll be headed out to the Kenai in a while for another day with guide Fred Telleen. My hands are sore and swollen from all the reeling. I've been using sunblock each day, but my skin is dry and sore as well. I find that if I put too much sunblock on later in the day, my eyes sting and tear. Will I ever get a good night's sleep?

Because I am up, I drive to the Russian River Campground and check to see if I can get into the site for a bit of very early morning fishing. No luck. There are at least fifty cars ahead of me, so I return to my room and sleep for another few hours. This fishing thing is ruining my health!

At 4:30 a.m. my alarm went off. I packed my stuff and vacated the room. At 5:30 a.m. I went to Gwin's Lodge, where I met Fred, who, by the way, is my favorite guide on the Kenai. Two other clients showed up and we were off. Fred is strictly a fly-fishing guide and if you don't feel comfortable with a fly rod, Fred will have you up and running with the pros in no time.

We put in at the ferry. I was thrilled to bypass the hordes that had amassed for the daily slaughter of fish. Fred paddled his guide boat as we floated for a mile or so downriver. Once again, I was amazed by the line of people standing just a few feet apart from each other fishing for the big one.

We found a quiet gravel bar and fished for a few hours. Each of us caught several handsome sockeyes. But this day, we were after rainbows. Fishing for "'bows," as they are affectionately called, in the summer is challenging. Normally, the big guys don't enter the river until the fall. But this was a different sort of year, out of sync with traditional ecological patterns. This was a banner sockeye salmon run. Usually, only seven to ten thousand sockeye enter the river. This year saw well over a hundred thousand running upstream. That attracts the crowds of fishermen, who fillet their catch right on the spot. Consequently, thousands of fish carcasses were dumped into the river, thus enticing the big 'bows and Dolly Vardens to enter the river early.

[THIS PAGE] *A case of dry files shows the variety of lures used on the quiet waters of Alaska.*
[OPPOSITE] *Battling a large rainbow on the Kenai can be the thrill of a lifetime. I've taken as many as a hundred trout a day.*

But still, fishing is not easy at that time of year.

To mimic what the trout may be eating, we fished with flesh flies that matched the colors of salmon tissue. I also tried my luck with black egg-sucking leeches, which had been productive for me several days earlier in a different part of the river. Even though we were required to fish with small, barbless hooks, we did very well fishing seams, drop-offs and ledges. We caught and released probably twenty or so throughout the day. They weren't huge, but who can argue with twenty rainbows over eighteen inches!

Fly-In

JUNE 19 This day started strangely. I had looked for a motel room the night before in Soldotna and everything had been at least $120 per night. I didn't need the Ritz; I just wanted a night's sleep without driving my charge cards so high that my wife would hit the ceiling! After some time, I found a new motel in Kenai for $50. No one had ever slept in the room! It was nice and quiet — perfect for a poor boy like me! Later that evening, I went to a movie and then had dinner.

I got up at 5 a.m., called home, checked all my gear and moved out of the room. At 8 a.m. I hopped on a 1956 DeHavilland Beaver pontoon and flew into the Chiliate River on the other side of Cook Inlet. We were met by an Indian who drove us some ten miles into the bush for a day of king salmon fishing. Upon opening the van door, we were literally attacked by billions of mosquitoes. They were dead serious about sucking our blood. They can make life really miserable.

There were five of us and one guide. The river was small, no more than twenty yards wide at its maximum. Four of the sportsmen turned out to be spinning fishermen. I was the only person using fly gear. The guide set me up in a small hole and said he would be back after he had situated the other fishermen. Every inch of the sandy bank I was fishing was covered with huge bear tracks and salmon carcasses. I hoped that I would not have company, at least not the kind with huge claws and four legs. I looked over my shoulder a lot and heard every noise. I had no inclination to wander off.

I've made the mistake of reading about grizzly bear attacks and my mind does tend to be imaginative. What I'm really saying is that it's easy to become obsessive about bears. You don't see many bears, but their signs are everywhere. I like seeing them from afar but not up close and personal.

I didn't see another person for over two hours. Why a guide would leave a client alone in the wilds of Alaska for that long, I will never know. It bothered me. I did, however, catch a great-looking twenty-inch rainbow. But I wasn't after trout — I was after king salmon on a fly rod. I had forty-pound leader material tied to the fly line and twenty-pound tippet connected to a large red salmon fly. I wanted a big guy. I wanted a real battle. Unfortunately, the kings weren't hitting flies that day. Eventually, I wandered from hole to hole and saw an occasional king roll. I wanted a big fish and would do whatever it took to catch one — I didn't want to kill it. There is honor in catching and releasing fish; there is no honor in killing something just to hang it on your wall.

The spinning guys hooked nine and landed five kings. The guide, right in front of me, even caught one. I tried everything from salmon flies of every color imaginable to leeches, spankers, muddlers, Chernobyl ants, nymphs, sculpins and everything else I could find on the bottom of my tackle box. I had no hits. I also felt abandoned by the guide, whom I saw no more than ten minutes throughout the day. I had also walked more than five miles downstream and then back again and carried more than forty pounds of gear with me through thick brush — with bears all over the place. I felt like the end of the experience had beat me up.

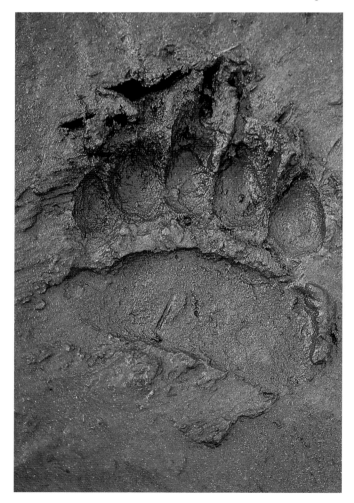

Very fresh brown bear tracks on the sand leave no mistake about who owns the shores.

It was a Prozac kind of a day. Fishing affects one's mental well-being. When the fish are biting, things are fine, but when they aren't, you might as well go into therapy, especially if everyone around you is catching fish.

I finally made it back to the van; we drove to the plane and returned to the lake on the Kenai Peninsula. I didn't tip the guide.

Fishing is funny stuff. You have to be able to take humiliation once in a while. It's not personal. You still have a life and someone out there likes you. Some days the fish bite and some days they don't.

That night I found my way back to Cooper Landing and had a great pasta dinner at Sackett's Kenai Grill. This old-world rustic restaurant overlooks stunning Kenai Lake and is complete with log tables with slab tops and really great food. The view from the dining room is gorgeous. It's my kind of place.

While eating dinner, I thought about the day and my reaction to it. Just a mile or so from our home in upstate New York, is the Double H Hole in the Woods Camp. It's Paul Newman's camp for terminally ill kids. I do volunteer work there and help raise money. I thought how selfish I was to be upset by the fact that I didn't catch my monster fish. Thinking about sick kids reminded me how blessed my life really is.

The Russian Again

JUNE 20   I had checked the guardhouse several times during the past few days, wanting to return to the Russian. It's just a few miles from where I was staying and I drove by there frequently. Each time many cars were waiting in line, and I had no desire to sit there for hours. At 3:30 a.m. this day, I was awake

BEAR LORE

I think about bears a lot. They are magnificent — no kidding. I've seen them from long distances and up close. I'm certain that I think about them too much. I have a paranoid tendency in my personality to think about things like this a lot. However, there is little danger from bears unless you do something stupid (like wander down a deserted dark road with three fresh fish in your pack).

Having spent time in fishing camps of all sorts, I have heard my fair share of stories. The best one I heard was at the Irma Hotel in Cody, Wyoming. One morning I was sitting with some friends talking about the wildlife in the area. At the table next to us was a man in his sixties, who, upon hearing us talking about bears, related the following story.

He had been a fishing guide for many years and had often taken clients on horseback into the mountains near the east entrance to Yellowstone National Park. These trips were usually one week long. One evening while returning to camp with his clients, the camp cook came running to him, shouting that he had just shot a bear with his .22-caliber rifle. Suddenly, the guide's horse bolted and threw him to the ground. He looked over to see a grizzly bear charging him at full force. He drew his .45 pistol and fired at the bear. The first shot paralyzed the bear's leg, but he kept coming. The next four shots hit him right in the head. The bear fell just twenty feet from the guide.

Bob Siter, owner of Gwin's Lodge Road House, plays a sockeye in the early morning hours on the Russian River.

Once the bear was dead the guide sat down at the campfire, had his evening coffee and then retired to his tent for sleep. It wasn't until the following morning that he started shaking from the events of the previous night. This went on for more than a day. Finally, he was taken to a hospital, where he recovered. The guide never went into the mountains again and turned to raising buffalo for a living.

I could see fear in the eyes of the man as he told this story. It was something I hoped I would never experience. It's far better, I have since thought, to watch bears on TV. ■

and drove to the entrance. There was no line! I paid my fee and drove up to the sockeye salmon parking lot, geared up and walked down to the river. As expected, there were hundreds of other fishermen lined up on the banks and in the water fishing. So without further ado, I jumped in at the first available spot.

After a half hour I hooked my first fish, which I lost. Then I foul-hooked a salmon that broke off all my fly line by running downstream in fierce water. I switched reels and continued fishing. People caught fish on either side of me, but I failed to land a salmon. In truth, thousands of fishermen had been taking thousands of fish out of the river for about ten days. The fishing was starting to slow down. And to be honest, I was tired. I wanted some peace and solitude. I was tired of the commotion and fishing lines flying everywhere. I was tired of the crowds and the fighting for fishing positions. I wanted to be with some friends and wanted to share the experience with someone I knew. I can only take crowds so long. I packed my gear, went back to my room and called my wife. I then took a badly needed nap for a few hours and worked on my computer for the rest of the day. Enough was enough.

Gwin's

In Cooper Landing, Gwin's Roadhouse Lodge is the center of the universe. Everyone goes there. They're open twenty-four hours a day during the fishing season. They offer a great traditional Alaskan restaurant that was built in the 1930s. If you go there, have a bowl of their salmon chowder. It's delicious.

The cabins at Gwin's Lodge in Cooper Landing, Alaska. Gwin's Lodge, including cabins, historic restaurant and store, is the cultural hub for fishermen in the area.

MOSQUITOES

If mosquitoes could be a billion-dollar business, Alaska could be the main supplier for this endeavor. There are so many of these nasty bugs in Alaska that you could easily use a bulldozer to harvest them. The only problem would be to find a consistent place to sell them. I know a mosquito business could work; I just haven't figured out all the angles yet.

Here on the Nushagak River I was finishing my morning coffee and counted almost thirty bugs on one of my hands, attempting to mercilessly suck my blood. They are ruthless, almost unstoppable, pitiless, vicious and disgusting. There are trillions of them. They will suck you dry and laugh all day long about it.

At night, if you don't have an adequate tent, their buzzing will drive you nuts as you try to sleep. And, unless you take really good aim, you'll wake up black and blue from swatting yourself in an attempt to hit the little buggers all night. They can find any hole or weakness in your tent. Nothing can be accomplished outside — not cooking, not going to the bathroom, not chopping wood — nothing — when mosquitoes are present.

I find no humor whatsoever inherent in these little creatures. Why they are on this planet is beyond me. They can never be pets; you can't take them for a walk, you can't pet them, they won't watch your house and they won't get a newspaper or fetch your shoes. They won't play catch or Frisbee, and they certainly won't keep you warm at night. They can also kill you by infecting you with more diseases than you can imagine. Stop and think about this: More than one hundred thousand people die each year from infected mosquito bites.

I hate mosquitoes, all of them.

We have devised all kinds of ways to stop them, but nothing works. These days we have insect repellents that are supposed to keep them off us. But just for a second read the labels on the containers of the best-selling insecticides. This stuff will lift varnish off furniture. You're not supposed to get it near your eyes or on open sores. You can have all kinds of allergic reactions to it, and it can kill you if you're not careful. It can also literally melt all kinds of plastics, such as fishing line and other gear. It's not good stuff!

But to be honest, I have a grudging respect for the bugs, as well. Mosquitoes are worthy of being nominated as the national insect. They are persistent, focused and innovative. They are creative in their capacity to solve problems (like getting into your tent or house). They are courageous and daring flyers, on par with falcons and fighter pilots. They can land anywhere and hang upside down for extended periods of time. In numbers, they are more powerful than any army the human race has ever devised. They can withstand almost any assault thrown at them and they keep coming. If I weren't a rational person, I'd swear that they were sent to terrorize us by some international group who wants the complete destruction of western civilization.

So, tonight I retire to my snake-proof tent, where I will sleep and swat at buzzing kamikazes whose sole intent is to make my life miserable. And they do a great job at that! ∎

June 20

JAKE'S NUSHAGAK SALMON CAMP

Again the lines
tangled and
I lost the fish.
Then three more
people butted in.

I was up at 3:30 in the morning. I called my wife

four time zones away in New York. She was making breakfast for our daughter, Lindsey. We talked of business and of my trip to Alaska. I owed her "big time," she said.

I geared up and drove back to the Russian River ferry and stood in line with about five hundred other fishermen. At 6 a.m., they opened the ferry and by seven I was fishing again on the Kenai. I found a great-looking spot and cast in. Within minutes several other fishermen were standing no more than four feet on either side. My line became tangled with theirs on the next three casts. "Sorry," was all they said. I hooked into a great salmon on my next cast, but again the lines tangled and I lost the fish. Then three more people butted in.

That was it. I'd had it. It was time to leave. I packed my pole, jumped back on the ferry and finally made it to my car. As I was packing up the vehicle, a game warden came over to inspect my fish. Since usually the only people who leave are those who have caught their limit, he was certain that I was concealing fish and searched my luggage and vehicle. I assured him that I had no fish and was just going home because I couldn't take the hordes of people anymore. "I don't blame you," he said. I left and went to Gwin's for breakfast. I will never again partake in combat fishing, at least not on this trip.

As I drove away from the river, I remembered being told that physicians from the local medical facility remove more than a hundred fishhooks a year from people fishing the Kenai. All the more reason to abandon the place, I thought to myself.

On my way up to Anchorage, I stopped at a small stream and threw a couple of casts in a small, picturesque vein of water, but found nothing. It was nice, however, to have the river all to myself: no people, just peace and quiet. From there, I drove to Anchorage and bought several items I would need for my trip the following day from a large tackle shop. After that, I found a Japanese restaurant in Anchorage and had a great sushi lunch.

From Anchorage, I drove almost all the way to Talkeetna, about two hours north of the city. Not a single room available anywhere. I drove back to Anchorage and the airport, where, I was certain,

[BELOW-LEFT] *A 1941 Flying Goose brings fishermen to Jake's Nushagak Salmon Camp on the Nushagak River in Alaska.*

one of the hotels would have a room. Still nothing. I finally found the last room available in all of Anchorage, $250 for the night. My wife would shoot me when the credit card bill arrived, but I was too tired to look further. I took the room.

The following morning, I drove around Anchorage and then finally made it to the airport for a 5 p.m. flight that didn't actually leave until 7 p.m. Once in the air, I took a short nap and was happy when I woke to find the plane in descent to our destination.

Dillingham, Alaska, is not really a city. It's a hard-core, working-class village of mostly fishermen, restaurant workers and blue-collar folks. The townspeople were mostly Native Americans, friendly and willing to talk of the town gossip and regional fishing. The roads were pitted with more potholes than the Ho Chi Minh Trail, and just about every building in the community needed a paint job. There were hundreds of boats in dry dock and old gear and machinery littered the town. But the people were friendly and the food at the Muddy Rudder Restaurant was excellent.

The airport itself was right out of the 1930s. Tiny and with absolutely no security checkpoints, Hollywood could not have created a more picturesque setting. Of the seventy-five or hundred people who were in the terminal waiting room, most of them wore wool work shirts, faded and torn blue jeans, boots, hunting jackets, pistols strapped to their hips, and hats of all shapes and sizes. These were rugged, fit men, right out of a Jack London novel.

The cars in the community were mostly beat-up wrecks. The windshield in the cab I took to my hotel was completely shattered and its interior was littered with trash and dirt. Only two of the five doors worked, there were no safety belts and the body had more dents and rust than Iraq's army after the Persian Gulf War. The cab driver spoke nonstop about fishing and insisted that I call him for daily updates on fishing the local waters. As if this weren't enough of an introduction to the village, at 5 a.m. an Indian character stuck his head into my first-floor hotel room via the open window and asked if I had seen George yet this morning. "No" was my only reply. He left and will never know how much he startled me. This sort of thing is not normal for me back home in New York.

In truth, however, this was my kind of place. The people were friendly and unpretentious. Even better, every store sold fishing tackle and everyone carried a fly-rod case.

I was only in Dillingham for an evening and a morning. I was there as a stop on my way to Jake's Nushagak Salmon Camp on the shores of the great Nushagak River. There I will do battle with the bears, mosquitoes and, on a fly rod, king salmon. I am incredibly excited about the event and look forward to true Alaskan wilderness and solitude, which I desperately need after my experience with combat fishing on the Kenai.

JUNE 23 After breakfast at the Muddy Rudder, I returned to the Dillingham airport and I boarded a plane right out of an Indiana Jones movie — a 1941 Flying Goose with an impressive new paint job. I was astonished that a plane like this was still in service. It was old — looked it and smelled it — and noisy beyond belief. It held seven passengers plus all our gear, which was loaded in the aisles, in the pontoons and other compartments. It shook like a serious earthquake when we took off. It wasn't pretty, but it did get us to Jake's.

Jake's camp had been established about twenty years earlier. Clients generally fish for all five species of salmon — king, silver, sockeye, pink and chum. Rainbows, Dolly Vardens and pike are also popular creatures to fish for in the river.

Happy clients with monster king salmon caught in the Nushagak River. Such fish are hard fighters and do not give up their lives easily. Many times fishermen will battle kings an hour before finally landing them.

Once we landed on the water and unloaded, I felt a bit out of place. It seemed that just about every one of the other twenty or so people in camp had attended this facility for years, and many of the fishermen hugged and greeted each other as old and trusted friends. Throughout my stay, I understood this better as the people attending the camp became like family members.

After we settled into our tents, we had a delicious lunch and then walked the ten or so feet to the edge of the Nushagak River for some early afternoon fishing. The camp was not really a fly-fishing camp, as most of the fishermen used long poles adorned with bait-casting reels, the easiest and best way to fish for kings in this setting. Nonetheless, each session some diehards like myself bring their fly gear and do battle with the king salmon that spawn in the river during June and July.

Throughout the five days in the camp, I generally fished from the shore. The tides brought new fish daily and it wasn't uncommon to land ten to fifteen kings a day. When the fishing was at its peak, several clients caught up to fifty kings a day.

But what I found most enjoyable about this camp were the other people. Their life stories were fascinating. One group of men in their eighties had camped somewhere on the water's edge each summer for the past twenty years. It was only the last four that they had attended a camp, as their physical disabilities required that they needed a bit of help with some of their activities. This group was affectionately known as the millionaires club. Each of the members was bright, articulate and charming beyond belief, like Norman Thayer Jr., the lovable and bodacious character brilliantly played by Henry Fonda in the movie *On Golden Pond*. Each had more stories than I thought possible, and each could fish with the best of them.

Whenever the millionaires club ventured onto a boat for a day's fishing, they brought along a sizable flask filled with their favorite spirits. Once they caught a fish, each man was required to have a healthy helping from the flask. They became the loudest group on the river. All of the other boats knew when they caught a fish because of their yelling and cheering. But they would land eight to ten big fish by morning's end, and by day's end would have had so much success, they had to be helped from their boat!

Another gentleman, Dave Plowman, who became my fishing partner, continually astounded

Fisherman Dale Suda struggles to show off a gorgeous king salmon.

me. On most occasions we would use exactly the same gear, fish in the same hole and stand side by side; yet, he caught ten times more fish than I did! I watched his every move and mimicked every detail of his presentation, but he still out-fished me!

People from around the world come to the camp. This season, a gentleman from Scotland attended. He used a fifteen-foot fly rod and bright flies and succeeded in landing many kings. An artist, he returned home with the intention of completing enough salable artwork to immediately return to the camp.

The kings in this river ranged from small jacks, three to eight pounds, to big bruisers up to fifty pounds. My largest, which was not very large, was about twenty pounds. My one moment of near glory came when I was hit hard on a long stretch of rocky beach. The rod bent and shook violently. I dreamed of a world-record salmon! The fish moved downriver and I followed it with my guide right behind me to help with the catch. The battle went on for more than twenty minutes. Because of the size of the fish, a small audience gathered to watch the fight. Finally, I was able to bring my monster close to shore. We all had a good laugh when we realized that I had been fighting a submerged, eight-foot log carried downstream by the current.

Jake Gaudet, owner of the camp and our guide for the five days I was there, also succeeded in looking foolish when he successfully landed a moose leg that he snagged on the bottom of the river.

Hank Wills, Bob Wills and Don Jensen proudly pose with a fresh-caught king salmon. All are over eighty years old and have fished together for the past twenty-four years.

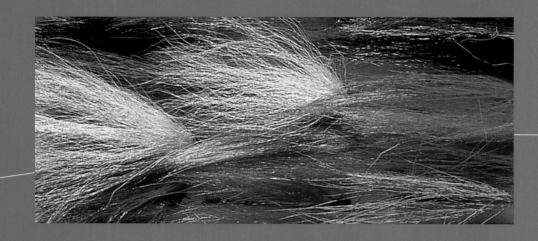

June 30

THE SUSITNA RIVER

Fishing
is better
than
marriage
counseling
any day.

Three days after my birthday, I was in Talkeetna, Alaska.

I needed some solitude and some real fishing. I was tired of kings, sockeyes, chums and big fish. I was tired of crowds. I wanted clear water and stunning scenery. I wanted a real Alaskan experience. I wanted the art of fly-fishing.

After speaking with several fishing guides in town, I hired a local water delivery service to take me up the Susitna River to a small stream called Clear Creek. This, I was told by the locals, would be exactly what I was looking for. So off we went in a metal jet boat to the "waters of promise."

Fifteen minutes later, I was shocked to see hundreds of fishermen and their tents in a two-block area, all fishing for kings. I was, to say the least, disappointed. I was also disappointed to see a silt-filled river with a class-two current that made wading nearly impossible.

But after wandering around a bit, I found Clear Creek. It was a tributary to the main river and the water looked promising. So up I went. To my delight, I found almost no people, and those who were there were salmon fishing.

I rigged my eight-weight rod with an egg-sucking leech and cast to a small bank ten yards from me. BAM! It was my first cast and I got a strike. It proved to be a gorgeous twenty-two-inch rainbow. I was thrilled! Ten yards farther upstream, I landed an eighteen-inch rainbow. I had stumbled onto a river of greatness!

When any species of salmon moves into a river, it displaces almost all of the other species. So usually the Susitna River is loaded with rainbows and Dollies, but they had moved to a smaller stream when the more aggressive salmon moved in. To carry this principle further, once the salmon spawn and are dying, the trout move back in and feast on the eggs and remains of the dead salmon.

For the next two hours, I stayed within two blocks of the main river. The fishing was superb and I saw no reason to move farther up the river. There were bears in the area and I had no great desire to confront one by myself. The town of Talkeetna, just a few miles down the river, had a serious problem with bears, and in 2001, five bears had to be killed because of confrontations with humans.

I caught three or four good-looking trout that day and released them all back safely to the stream. Later, I met my ride back to town and then departed for Denali and Mt. McKinley in the early afternoon.

The ride up to the country's highest mountain was stunning and uneventful. While traveling there, I fished a few roadside streams for graylings but was eventually pushed off the water by high winds and rain. I began my return trip to Talkeetna because of a poor weather forecast.

I had been up since 4 a.m. and was growing tired. The drive to and from Denali was about seven hours. I looked for a motel with vacancies but found none. The kings were in, and all the rooms in area hotels were taken, I was told. I continued to drive. Back in Talkeetna, I stopped at several B&Bs, hotels, hostels, cabins, motels and lodges. No rooms were available. It was now ten at night. I approached the owner of a lodge and just about pleaded with him for a room. The town was completely full, he said. He had even rented his own bedroom to a honeymoon couple so they could at least have a place to stay. But he did offer to let me sleep in his barn. "No charge at all," he said. I took him up on his offer.

The barn had no screens on the windows, no electricity, no plumbing and tons of mosquitoes. But it was a place to sleep and I could lock the door from the inside to keep the bears out. I moved in. It was at least dark. It was, in fact, the best night's sleep I had during my entire trip. I took a dip in the river in the morning and swam with the salmon as they made their spawning beds. The river was cold. Its source was melting glaciers. I did not swim long, but it did get my blood moving.

I went to town, had a delicious breakfast, fed the local dogs some biscuits I purchased in the general store and then made my way back up the Susitna River via the marine delivery service. The weather was clear and cool.

There were more people this time. It was Sunday. I wondered, at that time, if it were better to be in church thinking about fishing or to be out fishing thinking about church. I would leave the false humility answer to others.

I wandered up Clear Creek. There were fewer fishermen this time. I went past where I had been the previous day. The water was absolutely crystal clear and the banks were lined with massive, old-growth cottonwood trees. Four-foot ferns flourished as undergrowth. The cottonwoods were shedding their cotton-like spores. It was like a serious heavy snowfall.

A mile or so upriver, I caught a glimpse of another fly fisherman. He was in the water casting and his family was resting on the banks. I made several photos of him throwing his fly line. He knew what he was doing.

He was fishing about a hundred yards of bank that were lined with a few fallen trees and stumps. The shallow side of the shore was covered with new-growth willow trees about ten feet tall. I wandered into the water about seventy-five yards below him, where the water deepened to about five feet on the opposite shore.

Bam! I landed a fourteen-inch rainbow on a black egg-sucking leech. I made my way farther upstream. Bam! I caught another rainbow. The other fisherman noticed me and left the water. I moved close to him and caught another fish. Finally, I was right in front of him and his family, who were now sitting on the shore having lunch. We chatted for a few minutes and talked of fishing. "No luck, nothing today," he said.

I wandered back in the water. It was waist deep and cold. I cast a leech under a fallen tree and let the line drift. On the swing, the line stopped dead. I held on. The rod bent and started to shake. Fifteen feet from me, a huge, twenty-five-inch rainbow danced high on the water. It had my fly in its mouth. Again and again he jumped. The hook held, as did the knots. I backed to shore and handed the rod to the wife of the fisherman and asked her to hold the fish for a minute while I ran back to pick up my gear bag and camera. She had never seen such a large fish, she said. I made it back in a minute and made several photos of the fish. I was very pleased.

The other fisherman admitted that he had never seen such a fish and had had no luck on this very spot over the past few hours. I wondered how he and his wife felt seeing me land several trout on his spot right in front of him. We chatted for a while and I suggested that he try something black on his fly rod. I wandered back into the stream and fished a bit longer. The couple and their daughter left the area and the last I saw of them was as they turned a corner on the river. I hoped that he would catch a good

fish. It brightens people up and makes mar-
riages better. Fishing is better than marriage
counseling any day.

I wandered upstream for another three
hundred yards or so and wondered why no
one else was around. I continued to throw
flies and landed impressive fish frequently.
One hole under a submerged log produced
several twenty-plus-inch fish. I loved this
river.

Then I saw him.

Back down a trail between ten-foot-tall
willow trees he stood. He wasn't moving.
Huge, brown, virtually indestructible and
completely competent that he was the

Dolly Varden.

supreme ruler. I hoped that he did not see me as either a challenge or as food. My eye contact with
the grizzly lasted only a few seconds. I simply turned and resumed fishing. Then it dawned on me
that this was very, very real. I slowly wandered downstream. At about twenty yards, I turned back
upstream and saw no bear. He had stayed in the woods. I was a happy fellow. I continued a lot farther downstream.

A few hundred yards downriver, I mentioned to a few other fishermen that a bear was up above.
Apparently three young brown bears had staked out the river a year earlier and frequently made their
presence known. Usually, shouting or throwing stones at the bears was enough to run them off.
Fortunately, no major confrontations had occurred between these bears and the myriad of fishermen
that spent time in the area. Once the king salmon season ended and the fishermen were gone, the
bears had free reign of the area and could gorge themselves on fish carcasses.

I continued to fish the lower section of the river. I would not challenge the bear. When it comes
to brown bruins, I am a coward. I made definite plans to fish the upper section of Clear Creek later in
the fall.

That night I was incredibly fortunate to find a room in a lodge. I slept well and rose for a shower
at about three in the morning (remember, it's completely light at that hour in Alaska). At 4 a.m., I
drove back to the boat dock where I met a guide and three other fishermen. Once we were all loaded
on a jet boat, we traveled upriver for almost an hour. I had hoped for a secluded fly-fishing experience, but this would have to do. It was cold, the mosquitoes were biting and it was raining. But I
caught two big kings and several Dolly Vardens on a fly rod. It was a good day. We returned back
down to the dock at around 4 p.m. I said my good-byes and departed for Anchorage.

I found a motel room near the airport, slept for a few hours, packed my bags at 3 a.m. and drove
to the airport. Breakfast in the airport terminal was a banana at $1.59 and a cup of yogurt for $2.59.
I didn't think about the money. I would do that once the credit card bill came. At the appropriate
time, I boarded an airplane for the fourteen-hour ride home. It was a long day.

I would return to Alaska during the last week in August for the silver salmon run on the Tsiu
River. I knew my adventures would continue.

July 17

THE BUFFALO RIVER

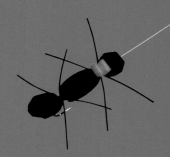

May
the spirits
guide me
to better
waters . . . .
I hate fishing.

We are in Moran, Wyoming

at an extraordinary estate I am photographing for a book project. The building and grounds are exceptional. A stone's throw from the back porch runs the beautiful Buffalo River. Meandering in the shadows of the Grand Tetons and situated about an hour above Jackson, the river has its own personality — rugged and complex. It wanders wherever it wants to go, ideal for wading and fishing. The banks are lined with grass and a deep trough runs down the outer bank insuring a safe haven for trout. There have to be fish in these waters.

But after four hours of fishing a hundred-yard stretch, nothing comes up. I see no fish rising and no signs of any hatch. I throw everything I have in the stream: wet flies, streamers, droppers' — you name it, I throw it. Nothing. As evening approaches, the mosquitoes attack with a vengeance. Wearing only a tee-shirt and waders, I lose easily a quart of blood. They are merciless.

This morning I drove to Jackson and visited a few tackle shops. I asked the right questions, including, "Why can't I catch any fish?" Apparently, the fish in the area are incredibly sensitive to water quality. They are known to move significant distances to more comfortable waters. The water in the Buffalo, I acknowledge, is stained brown. A few of the rivers in the Jackson area, including the Hoback and the Buffalo, have been subject to recent mudslides that have clouded the water, so the fish have turned off and moved out (just like my former wife!).

The river is well known in these parts and fished frequently by local guides. It is known as a quality fishery. With this in mind, I tried again this evening. In the water I went and threw dry flies, including Chernobyl ants and whatever else the confident young salesperson in the tackle shop had sold me. Nothing, not one swirl, hit, slam, rise, roll or jump. No fish.

The river ate a half dozen or more of my flies, and I returned to the ranch a beaten man. Poorer in both pocketbook and spirit, I sulked for a good ten minutes until I came to my senses. The scenery was beautiful. The Tetons glowed a dark red. Deer had drunk water on the shore just opposite from where I was fishing. Coyotes howled in the near background and the morning, just a few hours from now, would bring new waters. I am going to bed.

JULY 19   It's 5 a.m. How can I pass this up? What would I be if I didn't try? I look at the Buffalo River out my window. I look at my sleeping wife and daughter. Would they mind? I have to return. Otherwise, sometime in the near future I will wish I were fishing and curse myself for not giving it one more try.

I pull on insulated socks. Up comes my fleece long underwear. Out come my waders. They go on slowly and with effort. My muscles are a bit sore as are my ribs. Out of the corner of my eye, the sun creeps over the hilltops. The horses, cows, cats and dogs are stirring. Dew is on the grass. I put new flies in my vest. Life is short, I say to myself. I shall return. In the water I go!

Three hours later, the car is packed. Michele, Lindsey and Tina, Michele's sister, are anxiously sitting in the vehicle. I break down my pole and pack my fishing gear in the trunk. I vow to never fish again. I'm certain that I did something in a past life for which I am being punished by the fish gods. I'm also certain that not a single fish exists in the entire state of Wyoming. We depart for new territory. "May the spirits guide me to better waters," I say quietly to myself. I hate fishing.

But I'm stubborn and foolhardy.

Three miles down the road we see a turnoff for the Palisades River. I pull in. A communal groan comes simultaneously from the other three. "Just a couple of casts," I say. My wife rolls her eyes. Out come my waders, boots and fishing gear. I reassemble my fly rod and wander in. The water is cool and clear. I'm happy again.

With my first cast I get a strike! I'm a new man. Born again! A nice little fourteen-inch cutthroat trout.

Sensing the impatience in my family, I limit my fishing to only an hour. I pack my gear and drive into Jackson, where we eat lunch. I volunteer to take my daughter for a few hours while Michele and Tina go shopping. We agree to meet three hours later. Lindsey and I visit every fly-fishing shop and talk to every fishing guide in town. I hire a guide for the following morning.

When we meet again for dinner, my wife carries bags from her shopping spree. I'm sure everything she bought was on sale! "We really need these things," she says. "We really need to go fishing tomorrow," I say. She doesn't argue.

During dinner I develop a serious migraine. I get them once or twice a year and they're no joke. I excuse myself and walk to the motel where I take some medicine and go to bed. It's only 6:30 p.m., but I need sleep.

JULY 20   It's 6:30 a.m. Lindsey taps my shoulder and says, "Morning time, Daddy." I have slept heavily and don't know where I am. I roll out of bed, shower and make breakfast. By seven-thirty Michele and I are driving toward Victor, Idaho, where we will meet our fishing guide for the day. We arrive at the wrong shop, are told we don't have a reservation and leave. I have a very bad feeling about the day.

We find our twenty-one-year-old guide on the next block. It's the sixth trip of her career. While unloading our gear, I break the tip off my brand-new, expensive, nine-foot,

The beautiful Buffalo River, with the majestic Tetons as backdrop.

five-weight fly rod. I curse myself over and over.

We arrive at the headwaters of the South Fork of the Snake River, famous for its copious amounts of big cutthroat, browns and rainbows. I dare not ask my wife if I can use her eight-and-a-half-foot rod, so my only choice is a seven-foot, three-weight. I rig it up. It's windy out and I find I can cast the rod effectively for about ten yards. The river looks great and I settle in, resolved to make the best of the day. I find the fish are holding tight to cover. Precision casting in tight structure is the only way to get interest in my fly.

Within ten minutes a great-looking cutthroat slams my ant. I hold on for dear life. The rod bends like a piece of wet spaghetti, but the knots and the rod hold. I land the fish and have the guide hold the fish while I make a few photos, and we release the fish unharmed. Within the hour I catch a few others, including a lunker whitefish, which I happily lose at the boat.

Soon a violent storm stirs up. Rain forces us to shore, where we take cover for more than an hour. Hail stones slam through the trees, hitting us in the head. I lose my expensive new hat in the com-

motion. Since we are wearing shorts, we are soaked to the bone. The early morning clear weather did not necessitate the use of waders and rain gear. We shiver. The river rises and washes everything away. Mature trees float past us. This is not good.

The rain stops for a while and we begin to fish again, but it's useless. Shortly, the rains start up, as does the lightning, which strikes nearby. The skies are now ominously dark. We're in the middle of a wide river holding up metal-tipped fishing poles. The guide assertively tells me to put the pole down. We seek shelter again but are soon back on the river. We're now fishing several yards off the bottom of a five-hundred-foot canyon cliff. I hear rumblings from above. Looking up, I see a huge chunk of rock fall from the cliff top. It slams into the river twenty yards in front of us, literally coming within two feet of splitting a boat in half. The two occupants could have been killed. They quickly move their boat away from the cliff, as do we.

We are now shivering and cold. The water continues to rise. We arrive at the take-out and park the boat. Unfortunately, the person supposed to shuttle the cars forgot about us and the guide has to hitchhike back to the dam to retrieve her truck and boat trailer. It takes more than an hour.

Once she returns us to our car, the nut that holds the tow hitch for her trailer falls off. After searching for quite some time, it is finally found and secured back on the hitch. We arrived at our hotel at 8 p.m. Michele passed on going fishing with me tomorrow. I can't blame her.

JULY 21 I have renewed confidence and a rejuvenated spirit. Today will be better, I tell myself over and over. I drive back to the guide shop and meet up with two guides, Phil and Amanda, who have promised to take me to an isolated section of the Teton River. It's a long drive to the middle of nowhere. The vistas are extraordinary, the weather hot, the riverbanks rocky and the water warm. No one else is around. My first casts in a rapid pool are unproductive. We are using ants. I move downstream to quieter water. My fly gets hit each time on my first four casts. I then see Amanda fighting a large fish that she lands successfully. I decide not to make photos of the fish. It's still early and I assure myself that we will catch more.

I move upstream to fish near the second guide. I catch a small, eight-inch cutthroat. Then Phil lands a good fish. The pool we are fishing is deep. I switch to black egg-sucking leeches. I want to be on the bottom. I hook up a great eighteen-inch cutthroat — he is hooked well. I fight him for a few minutes, then call Amanda over to play the fish while I get my camera. The fish is still on the line when I return moments later. I make a few shots. When we are ready for a few close-ups, the fish pops off the hook and disappears. We'll catch more, I say to myself.

An hour later, Phil lands the largest whitefish I have ever seen. Although not high on the "desirable" list for fly fishermen, the fish is about twenty-four inches. I make a few good photos of the guide with the fish. Phil adamantly says that the fish is an embarrassment to his abilities as a guide and will ruin his career. "Too bad," I say, "Catch something better." He doesn't land anything else the rest of the day. Phil is actually a great guide. If you ever meet him, tell him how much you admire his ability to catch whitefish! I'm certain he'll appreciate it.

Soon the fish stop biting. We hunt them for a few more hours but then leave.

We drive for nearly two more hours to another section of the Teton River, this one more remote than the first. Parking the car, we descend more than a mile into a cavernous valley where a river is supposed to exist, finally find the water and wade in. This section of the river is the most difficult I have ever fished or waded, with a class-two and class-three water cascade down a rock-strewn valley. Fishing is difficult, as the water is fast and high. I have a few hits but catch no fish. We wade several hundred yards down the river. Amanda decides against going with us. She waits at the mouth of the stream. Wading is dangerous. We see fish rise in small pools but nothing hits the flies.

We wander back upstream. Amanda has caught two twenty-plus-inch cutthroats and has a larger one on the line. We fish for another hour but land nothing.

I can only describe the walk back up to the vehicle as murderous. In many places the pitch uphill is nearly ninety degrees. It takes us almost an hour to walk the mile. Matters are made much worse because I am wearing soaked waders and wading boots. I also carry a pack full of heavy camera gear. I have to stop every hundred feet to rest. It's tough to get old.

But I have failed to mention something else. I also have two broken ribs on one side and decreased lung capacity on the other, the result of surgery I had several years ago. All this is making for an absolutely miserable hour. I will say, however, that I would do the day over again in a second; the river is beautiful and the professionalism of my two guides obvious. But I am beat.

Exhausted and hungry on my ride back to Jackson, I stop at a small gas station in Victor, Idaho. They are having a sale on hot dogs and a large drink, which costs ninety-nine cents total. The dogs are delicious with extra onions. To top it off, I have a large ice cream sandwich for the ride home. Later I have the worst indigestion I have ever had. I will never eat gas-station hot dogs again. This experience brings new meaning to "EAT HERE AND GET GAS!"

Guides Phil and Amanda of World Cast Anglers landing trout on a variety of dry flies.

July 23

CORRAL CREEK RANCH

Once my
street shoes
were wet,
I just kept going
up to
my waist.

Casting on a small pond near the town of Ennis, Montana. On twenty straight casts I took twenty trout, including three that were over twenty inches! (Photo by Angie Puckett)

I was with Harry Howard of Yellowstone Traditions,

an incredible construction/design firm out of Bozeman, Montana. We were visiting one of his clients whose extraordinary ranch house was built by Harry's company. The ranch was located near the Madison River in Montana. After an extensive tour of the compound, we settled in for lunch. After we ate, Harry led me to a charming sod-roof house on the shores of a small stream-fed pond. "How about some fly-fishing?" Harry asked. His question was music to my ears.

Within minutes, we had unpacked our gear and assembled our rods. Be aware that this was an untouched and undisturbed natural fishing pond. The trout in the pond were natural to the creek that fed the pond. The owner of the property had never fed the trout. They were as natural and as indigenous as could be.

I rigged my rod with a light-colored dry fly (I had no idea what the correct name of it was!). First cast and Bam! A beautiful fourteen-inch cutthroat trout sent chills of excitement down my spine. With my second cast, a sixteen-incher slammed my fly but broke the line in the ensuing struggle. Every other cast produced a fish. I went for ten straight throws and landed a trout on each cast.

Harry had even better luck than I. His fish were eighteen inches and above!

Around five-thirty we broke down the gear and headed back to the main ranch house for dinner. Overlooking the Madison River and literally thousands of acres of stunning Montana mountain scenery, the private chef had created a wonderful barbecue meal for us. Before dinner, however, we were invited into an extraordinary log cabin that housed a full wet bar, pool table, and state-of-the-art electronic entertainment room. After cocktails and hors d'oeuvres, the owners of the compound and Harry and I ate a delicious dinner on the veranda. The full-time chef graciously served our meal, and we enjoyed the company of a wild pronghorn antelope that came within twenty yards of us. In total, the dinner lasted nearly three hours. Our host was an international mover and shaker who fascinated us with stories of huge business deals, political insights and insightful comments on such topics as corporate responsibility and the art world.

After dinner we said our good-byes to our hosts. I accepted a gracious invitation to stay at the ranch for three days the following week with my family. Once the car was packed and Harry and I were driving down the three-mile private road to the ranch, we noticed a secluded pond behind two fences a good mile off the road. I looked Harry right in the eye and said, "Real men fish!" He knew immediately what I meant. He stopped the car, I hopped out, unlocked the gate to the inner pasture and in we drove. A half-mile later, I opened another gate and we drove nearer to the pond.

We looked content and excited as we saw rainbows in the thirty-inch range slamming flies on the surface. It was just a few minutes after nine when we wandered in. I was not to be denied this experience so once my street shoes were wet, I just kept going up to my waist.

On my first cast, a small rainbow hit my line. Moments later, Harry's line was hit. After a ten-minute battle, his line broke. So we knew the fish were there, and we had permission to fish on the ranch whenever we wanted. It was dark and we decided to put off fishing the pond until the following week. We wandered back to the car, loaded up our gear and drove across the pitch-black Montana landscape.

Once outside the gate, Harry mentioned that he knew a shortcut through the mountains. It was at least two hours to Big Sky, where I was staying with my family, so a shortcut was welcome. Off into the night we drove and drove. After driving more than an hour on a winding dirt road, we came to a gate. Harry was certain that he knew the correct password to open it. After trying for more than thirty minutes, using every combination of the numbers he had written on his notepad, we passed through the gate and drove along the dirt road through the mountains.

Eventually we made our way into Ennis, Montana, and then to Big Sky. The trip back was four hours long. I was exhausted. I tried not to wake my wife and daughter as I struggled out of wet clothes and slid into bed.

The alarm went off two hours later at 6 a.m. I didn't know where I was, but Michele and Lindsey were shaking me with four of the most hated words in the English language: "Time to get up!"

[OPPOSITE] *Fisherman extraordinaire Harry Howard proudly shows off a Corral Creek trout.*
[THIS PAGE] *A gorgeous trout that is correctly known as Corral Creek trout. The fish was taken on a light brown hopper.*

As the sun set over the pond,
dramatic colors brightened
the Montana skies.

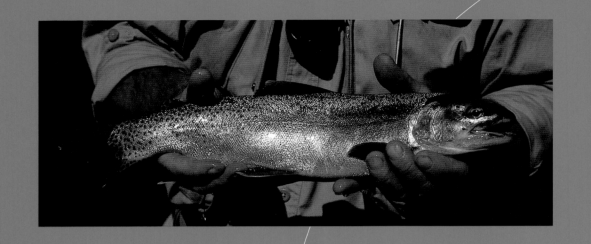

July 24

THE MADISON
RIVER

Fishing is
about
personal growth,
refining skills,
becoming
better humans.

Meandering Madison River provides home for elk, moose, bear and fish.

After a shower and light breakfast, we drove
to meet our fishing guide, Dave Olsen. On this day we would be fishing the
Madison River. Certainly one of the best-known rivers in the country, I had
fished the legendary waters many times and in different seasons. Bordered
by massive landscapes of rolling hills and mountains, the river is fishable
by either boat or shore.

A word of caution is warranted here. Earlier in the year a fisherman wandered into these waters to try his luck and skills. The Madison, although not a deep river, is stronger than it appears. Moving water can be treacherous. It can play havoc with one's balance and the river bottoms on which we are walking. We all want to believe that we are stronger and more experienced than we actually are. We all think that we are immortal and that accidents don't happen to us.

Unfortunately, the fisherman was swept away by the current. Although he was wearing waders, he did not have on a belt. A wading belt prevents water from filling up waders. Once your waders fill with water, you are in serious trouble. Tragically, the fisherman on the Madison lost his life in the incident. Please remember to use all your equipment properly and safely. On a further note, don't drink and fish, please. I'm tired of hearing and reading about unnecessary deaths.

With those thoughts in mind, we put the drift boat in at the public boat launch significantly downstream of Hebgen Lake and past the rapids which legends (and some guides) say hold huge browns and rainbows. The river was crowded that day. Maybe thirty boats had entered the water before us. Each boat had at least two fishermen. Each fisherman was experienced enough to know that trout love structure, holes and deep ledges.

But I want to back up a minute. My first experiences with the Madison came several years ago. It was back in my days with spinning rods. On my first trip down the Madison I was throwing Panther Martins with an ultra-light spinning rod. Seeing that every other fisherman on the water was fishing the banks, I threw my lures into the center of the river that had seen absolutely no pressure at all. On my first day I caught more than a hundred fish. And many of the fish were in the sixteen- to twenty-inch range. The guide couldn't believe it. But one right after the other, the fish hit my lure, fought like crazy and were eventually released back to the water.

I was told that whirling disease had devastated the rainbow population. I found that not to be the case at all. I caught huge rainbows again and again. And, surprisingly enough, I caught very few whitefish! I had fished the river for years with ultra-light gear and never once had a poor day. In truth — and I think everyone knows this already — if you want to catch tons of fish, spinning rods and lures are far more effective than fly rods. I will say that there is very little art to utilizing a spinning setup but fishing in that fashion can be fun and productive.

I should also mention, however, that the Madison fishes best in the late fall and winter. At that time, with a fly rod, I've caught huge browns and rainbows. There is very little traffic on the river and some guides will discount their prices during that time of the year. There are virtually no insects to drive you nuts. The fish at that time of year, however, hold tight to their structure and casts have to be right on the money.

Fly-fishing in the winter requires different rules altogether. It's critical that you dress properly. It can be very windy on the river. At the same time, any boat can tip over and you can easily fall in the water when wading. Further, gear has to be different. Tippet material has to be stronger because the line often runs over ice that can weaken and cut line. Ice develops on each eyelet of the rod and has to be constantly cleared. Nonetheless, fishing the Madison in late fall and winter can be extraordinary.

But things evolve and minds change. I'd fished the Madison for the last few years with my fly rod and had both good and mediocre fishing days. I no longer use my spinning gear. The art of fly-fishing has addicted me.

So on this day my wife and I were looking for a few huge fish and some great experiences. On advice from our guide, we were fishing mostly with dry flies with drop nymphs. Throughout the day we enjoyed the calm weather, the stunning scenery and fishing. Unfortunately, we caught mostly whitefish and a few good-size browns. We were satisfied with the day and the guide and knew we would return. Not all days can be extraordinary. One has to learn that with good also comes bad. We have far more poor to mediocre fishing days than we do excellent days. It's about paying your dues. It's about learning the art of fly-fishing and getting better at it.

Fishing is not personal. Fish don't congregate together and decide to make your life miserable. They just don't think or care about you. Fishing is not about greed or who has the most expensive gear or the best-looking outfit or who caught the biggest or the most fish.

A metal sculpture marks the western entrance to Ennis, Montana.

Fishing is about personal growth. It's about refining skills, cultivating ourselves and becoming better humans. It's about sharing knowledge and sharing experiences with those we care about. It's about rejuvenating ourselves so that we can tolerate, endure and overcome the drudgery that often permeates many of our lives. Fishing is a good thing. Life is short. It's necessary to remember that and to remind ourselves of how incredibly lucky we really are.

Don't beat up yourself because you lost a fish. Berating oneself is a sure sign of immaturity. Don't obsess on lost fish. We've all cursed ourselves for pulling the line too quickly, not letting the fish run and so on. Losing fish is an absolute guaranteed part of fishing. We've all seen someone break a rod or toss their fishing gear in the water because they lost a fish. That sort of behavior is inappropriate and just plain immature. Don't become psychotic just because you lost a fish. Learn from it and do a better job next time.

Relax a little, please. The only ones who profit from destructive behavior are tackle shops to replace gear, therapists and drug companies who profit when doctors prescribe Prozac or some other antidepressant.

So lighten up, relax and enjoy yourself. Before you know it you'll be sitting in a wheelchair thinking about all the stupid things you did as a youth.

[THIS PAGE-BELOW] *Brown trout taken on the Madison.*

July 28

THE SNAKE RIVER

Trophy fish
belong
in the
water
where they
were caught.

It is dark. The people are gone. Except for the ticking of the massive wall clock, there is no noise. The ticking is louder than one would think. The glow of the dark green light on my desk and the light from just a few wall sconces throughout the great hall is all that is visible. It grows quieter and darker by the minute. I've sat here many times at this hour but have never heard the cries that many say are real. To me, it's just a rumor to add mystique to the setting. The screams are supposed to come late at night from a child who died in a room while her parents ate dinner in the dining room. I hope I never hear her.

I'm on the balcony of the third floor at the Old Faithful Inn in Yellowstone National Park. It's 1:30 in the morning. I'm overlooking the balcony now and marveling at the structure. For me, this is a holy place. Certainly the finest historical example of a "log cabin," the structure has withstood the ravages of time, forest fires and natural elements. I love the place. I've been here many times and proposed to my wife here. I would rather be here than anyplace in the world.

I'm still thinking of my experiences just two days before and wondering if they were real. The fishing had been slow during the past two weeks. I had tried my favorite fishing haunts, including the Madison, South Fork, the Teton, the Gallatin and several other spots, but the fishing remained slow. The waters were muddy and hot, forcing the fish to think of other things besides eating.

This past Thursday I had called my good friend Keith Shorts, who is a fishing guide, and we talked

[THIS PAGE] *The Snake River offers fishermen hundreds of ripples, eddies and drop-offs that all seem to hold fish.*

[THIS PAGE] *The South Fork travels through rugged terrain and mature trees. Utilized not only by fly fishermen, rafters and white water enthusiasts enjoy the clear waters of the northern Rocky Mountains.*

[OPPOSITE] *Signs in the area of Jackson, Wyoming, indicate that fly-fishing is a significant industry in the region.*

about the waters. Keith has been a long-time resident of Jackson Hole and invited me to fish with him the following day. I had fished with Keith on many occasions over the past seven years and have come to realize he is the quintessential guide. His absolute attention to detail and prodigious knowledge of the rivers is what makes him so great. Besides being a great fishing guide, he is genuinely a great person as well!

He wanted to fish the "in town" section of the Snake River and, of course, I accepted his invitation. In the morning we met at the Wagon Wheel Resort where I was staying with my family. Unfortunately, we couldn't find a baby-sitter, so Michele would spend the day shopping and entertaining Lindsey. It had rained heavily throughout the night and the clouds were still ominous as we packed my gear in Keith's vehicle.

Not wishing to get caught in a serious storm, we decided to do some bank fishing on the Gros Ventre River (pronounced grow VAUNT). As we drove into the almost obscure pioneer town of Kelly, Wyoming, just about a half hour north of Jackson, I asked about the price of a tiny log cabin that had a "For Sale" sign prominently posted near the street. My wife and I had considered buying a small place in the area and the cabin before me seemed ideal.

"That house is presently listed at $840,000," said Keith. I asked him to repeat his statement. "Eight forty is what they want, Ralph." To me, the house should have been around $60,000, but prices in the Jackson, Wyoming, area defy comprehension. I knew I would not be making an offer on the house that day.

Soon we were wading in the Gros Venture. On the advice of Keith, I fished with a small black-and-red Chernobyl ant. "Yellowstone cutthroat trout love red," Keith said. The fish were holding tight, I was told, but on my first cast I nailed a beautiful eighteen-inch cutthroat. I was thrilled. The ice was broken. I had several other hits within the next half hour and managed to land a few. Keith had also landed a few smaller fish but nothing major. About that time, the skies cleared up and we both quickly agreed to float the Snake just outside of Jackson.

Within the hour, we were floating down the river, throwing flies against rocks, in seams, eddies and all kinds of hydraulics. In general, we stuck with dry flies and had switched between ants, PMDs, stone flies, Wulfs and other surface lures. Because they attract too many small trout and whitefish, we did not use nymphs at any time. Throughout the day, we caught several fish on the Snake, each exciting and beautiful in its own right. I was not in the least disappointed.

Once we were through with the Snake, Keith mentioned that he wanted to try one more stream. I couldn't say "no." So we packed our gear and hiked more than a half hour to a small stream that I was certain would hold some great-looking twelve-inch fish. The stream's maximum width was not more than thirty feet at any point. It appeared no more than three feet deep at any place. The water was perfectly clear. There were no other shoeprints or telltale trash that might have indicated other visitors to the area. The banks were mostly covered with short vegetation and small willow trees. Further, the region was home to a herd of more than thirty elk; their hoof prints were everywhere.

Our first spot was a small rock ledge that featured a small eddy. I had three strikes on four

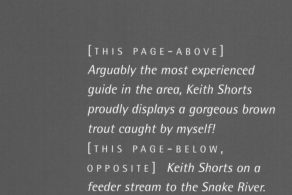

[THIS PAGE-ABOVE] *Arguably the most experienced guide in the area, Keith Shorts proudly displays a gorgeous brown trout caught by myself!* [THIS PAGE-BELOW, OPPOSITE] *Keith Shorts on a feeder stream to the Snake River.*

casts. The fish were small and the fly was too big for them to grab. We moved upstream about fifty feet. With Keith standing right next to me, we quietly approached the setting. I made my first casts about thirty feet above us. We were standing about eight feet away from the shore. We did not want to spook the fish.

With the first cast there was nothing. At the fifth cast, there was still nothing. With a tenth cast to exactly the same spot, there was still nothing. During all this time, Keith was coaching me on my technique and insisted that I continue throwing to this same spot. His comments included suggestions on how much line should be out, the correct mend, which side of the channel I should be throwing on, stripping and other things. Keith is a master (I'm not kidding) at this kind of stuff and I considered all his advice.

To be completely honest, I am a high-energy guy with the attention span of a three-year-old. After three or four casts to a spot no wider than ten feet across, I felt the pressing need to move on. But Keith is persistent and patient. "Cast again, Ralph," he kept saying. And there would be nothing. "Again," he said. I cast.

Then IT rose from the deep. Its mouth was wide enough for my entire fist. Its color was a dark, golden brown. It sucked in my fly like a whale on anchovies. My rod bent and shook. My dream fish was on my line. I had him.

Now, being a veteran with a fly rod, I am smart enough to know that one does not manhandle a

[ABOVE] *During the past few years the rivers in the area have been subject to drought-like conditions thus causing water to be very low. Under these circumstances, however, trout find deep holes to wait for the next rain.* [RIGHT] *Guide Keith Shorts casts to waters below a dam on the Gros Ventre River.*

fish into submission, especially when you are using light line. Let the rod do what it's designed to do. The fish peeled line off my reel. First twenty yards, then thirty yards. I did not fight with it. The fish would tire, I said to myself. Let the drag do the work. Ten minutes later, I landed it on the bank. I was elated. A twenty-one-inch unscarred Yellowstone cutthroat trout was mine. No one could ever take that away from me. And on a dry fly!

We made photos, admired it and released it quickly and safely back into the stream. At that moment, I was completely satisfied. It was the largest "cut" I had seen in a while, let alone landed. I was ready to celebrate and felt invigorated with enough new energy to tolerate the half-hour "bushwhack" back to the truck. It was now 6 p.m. and I couldn't wait to tell my wife! And I had photos to prove it!

But Keith was in no hurry to return. "Try it again," was all he said. So we approached the stream and I cast to exactly the same spot. This time "grandaddy" let himself be known. Huge, monstrous and beautiful, he hit like a Mack truck, and with the same fly and same presentation. He only jumped once. The water was so shallow and so clear that we could see him perfectly — dark, brown and beautiful. He took line off my reel at his will. I could only "palm" the spool to slow him down. I was using four-pound tippet material and was determined not to lose him by trying to "horse" him to shore.

Shortly, he ran downstream and tangled himself on a tree stump. "That's it," I said to myself. I was certain that was the end of him. But fortunately, Keith entered the water just below the stump and startled him into returning upstream. He untangled himself. I reeled like mad. Past me he went. The line and the knots held. Keith tried to net him, but my sixteen-inch net was worthless. In time, he too tired and I brought him close to shore. Time and again he revived himself and took line from my reel.

Soon, however, we were able to land him. He was twenty-four inches, golden brown and perfect all around. I was thrilled. Words were inadequate to describe the moment. Keith was thrilled for me. A great guide is ecstatic when his clients catch supreme fish. We released the fish back to his home, exactly where he belonged. Trophy fish belong in the water where they were caught — not on some wall. Trophy fish are the breeders who have the capacity to re-create more trophy

fish. It's both ecologically wrong and immoral to kill them. Respect for life is the highest form of humanity. Hang photos on your wall, not dead things.

But Keith wasn't done yet. We moved downstream. Not far, mind you, just twenty yards or so. BAM! First cast and another great fish was on the line. This time I handed the rod to Keith. I wanted to make photos of the action and I knew he would not lose the fish. Ten minutes later we landed another twenty-plus-inch fish. Again, we made photos and released the fish.

Over the next half hour, we hooked up with two more monster trout. Without either of us being the least disappointed, both fish broke off from the line. It was okay. No person could have had a better day fishing than I. Later, we returned to the vehicle and made it home. Both Keith and I were like two little kids.

In retrospect, I realized that an exceptional guide not only puts you on fish but also leaves you with new skills and information. Art, they say, is in the details. Great fishermen are artists. And great guides help other fishermen become better.

And so it's been raining all night here at the Old Faithful Inn. It's now about 4 a.m. The sound of rain on the ceiling is pervasive. Not a soul has passed my desk for more than an hour. I do hear the occasional groan and creaking of expanding logs that make up the inn. Settling logs act that way. I haven't heard the cries. I prefer to think of fishing. Life sometimes is good. No life is perfect. We all need bright moments to brighten our days. That's what gets us through the hard times, the mountains and valleys. That's the way it is.

The Gallatin

The next afternoon we left Old Faithful and traveled north to Big Sky, Montana. I was incredibly disappointed to find that the rivers in Yellowstone, including the Fire Hole, Madison and Gibbon, were closed to fishing. The weather had been horribly hot and a major fish die-off from water more than eighty degrees had killed hundreds of fish. Best to leave the remaining fish alone was the thought of the day.

Nonetheless, the drive through the park was still thrilling. Elk, bison, deer and eagles were everywhere, and the young trees that had grown since the fires of 1987 were filling in the hundreds of thousands of acres that had

[OPPOSITE] *The Snake, which gets its name because it wanders all over the place, is known for its cutthroat trout; the river offers both advanced and beginner fishermen the opportunity to catch and release more trout in one day than just about any other river in the Lower forty-eight!*

burned. Still, the snags and carcasses of the burned trees reminded me again how everything can change with just a few moments of carelessness.

Once in Big Sky, we settled into a stunning home that a friend had loaned me for a month. That evening, we ventured down to the Gallatin River and threw a few flies into fishy-looking areas. As the evening progressed, fish were rising. Nothing huge, mind you, but good-looking fish just the same.

I was throwing hoppers, but nothing large enough to make the fish hit my line. I switched to brown stimulators and a drop nymph, but still no takers. I changed to a very small light brown "thing" and landed a small trout. Then I switched to a small black streamer and landed another small trout.

The trouble with all this was my inability to think like a fish and to act like one. The study of entomology is critical to the evolution of a fly fisherman. Fish simply will not eat anything outside their normal eating patterns. If you cannot discern between a caddis fly and a mayfly hatch, your chances of catching fish are greatly diminished. Knowledge is power. There is no other way to put it. On my way home that evening, I vowed to spend time reading about bugs.

Again, the Gallatin

AUGUST 3 I spent the morning on the Gallatin. I fished a stretch just out of Big Sky. It threatened rain all day and was windy. Before I fished I went to the fly shop and asked what the fish were hitting. The salesperson assured me that the fish were in a pattern where they were eating absolutely nothing other than size-eighteen prince nymphs off two-pound tippet. The flies had to hang

at least twenty-four inches below a strike indicator made up of pink yarn smothered with a floatant called gink. Okay, so I bought all the stuff and rigged my line exactly the way I was told. I fished for almost two hours with my "guaranteed gear" that I tied correctly and fished exactly the way I was told.

Nothing at all hit my line. No big fish, no little fish — not even a snag — nothing.

I switched to a trusty black egg-sucking leech and started catching fish. First a few small, good-looking rainbows, then I landed three sixteen-inch fish in quick succession. I ended the day by having a great twenty-inch fish on line but lost him in current when he jumped and spit the hook right in my face.

Later that day the wind increased dramatically and then it started to rain. I was finished by 3 p.m. On my way

back to my "estate" I stopped by the fly shop to pick up some extra tippet material.

"How was fishing?" the salesperson asked.

"Great," was my only reply.

"Did you fish the prince nymphs the way I told you?"

"Sure did."

"Well, how did you do?"

"I caught about eight, including three sixteen-inch fish, and I nearly landed a twenty-incher as well."

"I told you the nymphs were the only way to catch fish on this river," the salesperson said.

I quietly paid for the line and left.

RUMINATIONS

Lately, in the circles of fly-fishing, there has been significant discussion on the differences between quantity and quality fly-fishing. On several occasions I have had friends comment that they had no desire to jump into a combat fishing scene and partake in the catching of fish.

At its highest level of perfection, fly-fishing is a profound art form. This is no different from intense involvement in any activity. Where skills become perfected, quality is pursued and the refinement of motor skills becomes apparent. Art happens.

With time, a deep appreciation for the activity occurs.

Although I partake in the activity, I don't consider most combat fishing an art. It is nothing more than the active process of acquiring meat for the freezer. Although this is not meant as a criticism of those who participate in the activity, and the sport does have its moments of art for some, for me there is something uneasy and unsettling about the activity.

Once an individual has acquired a level of artistic competence in the realm of fly-fishing, they have to have developed an unmistakable and undeniable basic respect for the life of the fish. Without this, the entire activity becomes nothing more than mere physical activity and the constant pursuit of survival. Basic respect for life, whether it is bears, fish or humans, is the highest achievement of human existence. With little or no respect for the lives of others, one's own life is cheapened.

I'm a simple guy. My style of fly-fishing is the best example of this. I use the simplest flies available. And as long as they're black, I'm okay. I love black egg-sucking leeches and black woolly buggers. Get 'em down near the bottom and I'll catch fish. Once in a while I'll hang a drop nymph off the black fly, but for me, the simpler the better.

Some of the guides I've fished with over the years amaze me. They can pick out a dun from a boogie fly at fifty yards. They can identify every insect alphabetically that has emerged on any river in the United States. They know more than professional entomologists. I'd swear they're in love with bugs.

And fish boggle my mind as well. I was fishing with a guide at the confluence of the Snake and Hoback Rivers about a half-hour drive south of Jackson, Wyoming. It was a gray, cool, shady day. Around 10 a.m. we started seeing lots of activity. Fish were rolling in pockets off rocky outcrops. The water was clear and we could see them as they began their ascent to gobble up a hatch of caddis flies one at a time.

So we switched to caddis flies and cast right into the center of activity. After first and second casts, there was nothing. We backed off a bit and allowed for longer swings on the drift, but still, nothing. We switched to size-eighteen hooks, the smallest flies we had with us. We changed colors and switched to two-pound tippet material, and still there was nothing. And yet there were fish all around us slamming flies, just not ours.

There is nothing more challenging to a fisherman than to see fish all over the place and not being able to get them to bite on your line. So we switched from a caddis fly to an emerging caddis fly. In truth, I could not see the difference. An emerging fly is incredibly subtly different. Average guys like myself could never pick it up without being told. Further, the flies were so small I swear one would need an electron microscope to tie the dumb things on the end of a line. Finally, one has to consider that the water where the fish were rolling was not only foamy but rapid as well.

So I cast in the water and got a strike! A beautiful sixteen-inch rainbow nailed my line. I didn't horse it as the line was so thin that I doubted that it would hold in rapid water. But I landed it!

After the second cast, there was another fish. Then another after the third cast, this time, a cutthroat trout, and a real beauty.

Soon I got the hang of it. Once the fly hit the water, it was no more than two seconds before a strike occurred. The best way to catch them was not to watch the fly but the water within three feet of the fly. With polarizing glasses one could see the fish start their run. It was all a matter of timing. Once the fish were near the fly, it was only a matter of a very soft hook set to get the fish on the line.

Fish are incredibly perceptive. They are marvels of evolution capable of surviving and thriving in very hostile waters. Their brains are tiny, but they know enough to have been able to survive for some hundred million years. They deserve more respect than they get.

BACK TO CORRAL CREEK RANCH

I've been
to the top
of the
mountain
and life is
good there.

For the past three days I've been photographing

an incredible estate in southern Montana. Running through their property is tiny Corral Creek. In absolutely the middle of nowhere, this creek would have a hard time getting the time of day from a thirsty crow. The creek is so small, one would never think that it could support life of any kind, but it has its own brand of fish! State ichthyologists have declared Corral Creek cutthroat trout a subspecies all its own. Darker than normal cutthroats, they have a unique way of hitting dry flies. I'm serious when I say I caught literally hundreds of them during my four-day visit to this private estate. Instead of slamming the flies from underneath, they jump out of the water about a foot from the fly, then hit it on the downward leg of their assault. It was fascinating to watch. This is certainly not a new approach for trout, but it is unusual for so many to use this approach; I will say that 99 percent of the fish I caught took the flies in this method.

So in the evening and early mornings I've been fishing a small pond no more than a quarter of an acre large. Each time I fish it, I have a hit on every cast and land a fish on every other.

On the evening of July 29, the owners of the estate suggested that I try the swamp. I had fished this area a week earlier with my friend Harry Howard but decided to give it another go. At 6 p.m. I drove to the pond, opened the two livestock gates and wandered alone to the shore. Badger holes were everywhere and a mature bald eagle screamed at me. This was obviously his fishing hole and he hated intruders. He also probably had more luck than I did, because I wandered in and fished for more than an hour before I had my first hit.

I was surprised that I saw no rising fish throughout the entire evening even though there was a hatch going on. Eventually, the only way I caught fish was on streamers with a heavy weight on the line to get down toward the bottom. Unfortunately, the fish were in the middle of the swamp. I had to wade nearly chest-deep to finally get some action on my line, which actually scared me. I had fallen once on unstable ground and injured my leg. I had carried a large black-and-blue mark on my thigh for more than a week as a reminder of the incident. As I was alone and had no desire to step into an abyss in the middle of nowhere with no one around, I backed off. I did catch probably fifteen beautiful fat rainbows in the twelve- to fifteen-inch range, but feeling uncomfortable in the deep pond by myself, I wandered back up to my original fishing hole, the mountainside pond.

The entire experience was a most beautiful and extraordinary evening. As I fished the small pond, a herd of pronghorn antelope came and drank. They knew I was there and watched me closely before quenching their thirst. Then a deer and two fawns stepped out from the bushes no more than ten yards from me and drank. They spent a good half hour watching me before they took off.

I was using a large, brown hopper with a barbless hook and had a hit on every cast. A few of the fish were small, but the ones I landed were in the twelve- to sixteen-inch range. It took nearly ten minutes to land the largest, more than twenty inches long! I released all the fish, unharmed.

Eventually, the sky turned a bright pink and then faded as the sun sank lower and lower behind the mountains. As I watched the pond, the surface was broken by the rolling and jumping of hundreds of trout feasting on a nightly snack of mayflies that came from the bottom of the pond to finish their short lives.

A pack of coyotes (they could have been the wolves that had made a dramatic comeback in Yellowstone Park next door) howled in the background. As nighttime took over the earth, stars of incredible brilliance took over the skies.

I live a fantasy life. I fish just about every day. I stay at many of the greatest rustic homes in the world. I write books, play music and make my living in the art world. I am thankful for my blessings. I've been to the top of the mountain and life is good there. Soon I broke down my gear and returned to my wife and daughter in the guest cabin. ⌒

This gorgeous trout is correctly known as Corral Creek trout. The fish was taken on a dry fly.

August 1

R U B Y   L A K E

The mere
thought
of the
land can
take one's
breath away.

We packed the car and were on the road by 7 a.m.

We drove for about an hour to the small fishing town of Ennis, Montana. We had a quick breakfast at the drug store and then left Lindsey at the local daycare center. She needed to play with kids her own age, as she was sick of us "old folks."

We met our guide, Dan Dee, at the Madison River Fishing Company. Dan is a long-time friend of our hosts at the Corral Creek Ranch and was reputed to be a great guide with a profound sense of humor. We were not in the least disappointed. At first we were on our way to "do" the Madison, but Dan stopped alongside the road where we rethought our day and decided to head down to Ruby Lake.

Within the hour, we were safely paddling across a smooth, glassy body of water. I watched the horizon carefully and saw no rising fish. Large weed beds seemed to choke the lake. Pelicans, seagulls, geese and ducks flew and paddled about.

We fished for almost an hour with no results. We fished with small, tapered, leech-looking flies at the ends of our lines. Considering the shallowness and clarity of the water, I personally would have thrown either dry flies or dragged a black woolly bugger along the bottom. Dan also fished with a tiny size-eighteen nymph tied just a foot below a piece of yarn. I worried about our fishing techniques, but I swore long ago to always do what the guide says. So I persisted.

We moved the boat to another section of the lake. This time Dan hopped out of the boat into nearly four feet of water. We were at the mouth of a stream and could see big fish rolling. I hopped in right after him. Using the tiny flies and bits of yarn, we threw upstream and stood patiently while the slow current dragged our bait away from us.

Fifteen minutes into the experience, we had our first strike. Dan landed a gorgeous sixteen-inch rainbow. Light in color and in perfect condition, the fish was a beautiful subject for a photograph.

Both Dan's guiding and teaching techniques were above questioning. Throughout the day we talked of not only the local area and fishing but of running a small business and headaches encountered in such endeavors. Dan had recently retired and was living the good life in Montana. He caught significantly more fish than I, but, then, professional guides of great experience usually do. This is their water and their country. But I learn quickly. I had always encouraged guides to fish as watching them has been both educational and enlightening; besides, I'm not a greedy guy and if the fish are biting, why not?

I missed my first five strikes. Fishing with tiny, barbless hooks has always been a mystery to me. If one pulls too hard or attempts to set the hook too aggressively, there is a high probability of displacing or dislodging the hook. It's far better to gently lift the rod and let the hook do the work. This is a technique easier spoken of than actually practiced.

I soon got the hang of it. I landed several beautiful rainbows and was proud of the fact that I had seen and learned a few new techniques. Just about all of the fish we caught throughout the day were caught while we were wading. Every once in a while I stepped into a hole and came within an inch of the top of my waders. I had no desire to sink myself, so I was cautious.

The evening came and we said our good-byes to Dan "the man." He invited Michele and I to fish with him anytime, and we acknowledged that we would someday accept his offer. On the ride toward

Guide Dan Dee casting on the glassy waters of Ruby Lake.

Big Sky, Montana, where we were staying, we stopped at the Grizzly Bear Restaurant and had a great dinner overlooking the Madison River.

Montana is one of the great treasures in North America. It would be easy to exploit the area with shopping malls, fast-food restaurants and "el cheapo" motels. It would be easy to stock the rivers with so many trout that just about anyone could catch a fish. It would be easy to develop cheap housing and make a bundle. It would be easy to cut the trees and dig the land and spoil the clean waters.

But I hope that civic leaders somehow find the courage and foresight to discourage and prevent developers and money mongers from spoiling further regions of this expansive land. The settings here are so glorious and wonderful that the mere thought of the land can take one's breath away. Peace and beauty throughout the country are not an awful lot to ask. I want my daughter and future generations to be able to experience the settings that I have been enthralled with. I cannot say thank you enough to the early guardians of our great country who set aside the land that today is Yellowstone, Gallatin, Teton, and many other national parks. They had more courage than many of the people alive today. Their efforts shall forever be remembered.

August 10

THE BIG HOLE RANCH

We
are all
hunters,
whether we
like it
or not.

I had been wandering around Montana

for the past three or four days just exploring. Once people hear that you are a writer, they want to tell you all their stories. Not only about fishing but about their operations, their grandkids, their horses, the prices, local politics, their wife or husband, their neighbors and anything else that comes to their minds. Fortunately, they occasionally want to tell you about their favorite fishing spots. I had fished here and there and just about any other place that was recommended.

The state speed limit is seventy-five miles per hour, which means that everyone — and I mean everyone — drives eighty-five and many drive ninety-five miles per hour. Now, eighty-five miles per hour is very fast, and when people pass you on the road, you sort of wonder what's going on.

One of those days, after a few hours of white-knuckle driving, I stopped in a tiny town for lunch. I had no idea the name of the town or where I was. Quiet and significantly out of the way, it seemed just like the kind of place where I could relax. As I drove through town, dogs barked, men on horseback waved and old men sat in front of the hardware store in cowboy hats. Two storefronts had "For Rent" signs in them. The Conoco gas station still had full service. It was my kind of place.

I pulled into a parking place in front of a great-looking saloon that said "EAT" in weathered blue letters above the entranceway. Old Chevy trucks with rifle holders in their rear windows and dogs sitting in the flatbeds lined the street. A horse trailer, complete with horses that snorted and stamped their feet when I came too close, stood nearby. The laundromat was full of people washing their clothes. I walked into the saloon for an afternoon lunch.

Gambling is completely legal in Montana. A card table was set up and a professional card dealer was sitting at the table. I had never seen anyone as stone-faced as him. I'm an emotive, smiley kind of guy, so I said, "Howdy." He nodded back without breaking a wrinkle on his face — not a smile, not a word, nothing but a stone-cold poker face. I walked on by.

As I looked around, I couldn't help but notice the ambiance of the place. Real cowboys with real cowboy boots. Real cowboy hats. One guy actually had on chaps and spurs. They were all sitting at the counter smoking hand-rolled cigarettes and sucking on long-neck bottles of beer. An old gray dog slept in the corner and Dolly Parton songs played on the jukebox.

I took a seat at a table directly behind the cowboys. I wanted to hear their conversation. I was certain they were talking about cowboy stuff like horses and women and round-ups and rodeos and branding irons, just like in the movies. After about ten minutes, I heard a phone ring. One of the cowboys pulled a cell phone out of his vest pocket.

"Harry here," was all he said, and then after a few minutes, "Bill, I'm concerned about the direction of all this. I want you to sell all my shares of AT&T. I want the funds split between blue chipper Microsoft and Johnson & Johnson. And I hear Merck has a new drug coming out, so buy me a hundred shares of Merck. Call me back to confirm. Thanks." Then he disconnected.

A few minutes later another "cowboy" got on his cell and called his office. Apparently he was the local dentist. One other cowboy called out to the waitress, "Gloria, honey, bring Bill another latte here, will you please. Heavy on the vanilla." Things just weren't what they appeared to be.

I ate my buffalo burger, finished my drink, nodded to the card dealer and left. My heart was broken. My dream that real cowboys do exist had ended. Life would never be the same for me. I vowed to watch a few reruns of *Hopalong Cassidy* and *The Lone Ranger* that night in my motel room.

I drove about three hours south on I-15 to the almost-nonexistent town of Melrose, Montana, located on the banks of the Big Hole River. A guy I had met a few days earlier had suggested I fish this river and given me exact directions. It was now evening. Wearing only wading shoes, shorts and a fishing vest, I entered the stream and fished for almost two hours but caught nothing. A small hatch of something was coming off the river and I unsuccessfully tried my best to match it. I spent the night at the Sportsman's Motel and had breakfast at the Hitching Post restaurant in the morning. I returned to the river and fished for another hour, but there was still nothing.

I went into the Sunrise Fly Shop next to the motel and restaurant where I met Kristie Piazzola, owner of the fly shop and apparent queen of the Big Hole River. I spent a good hour there bantering with her about all sorts of stuff. She is a real sweetheart. She could beat me at anything. She even talked me into buying a bunch of flies I was certain I did not need, would never catch fish with and that would, no doubt, lie in the bottom of my tackle box in perpetuity. I even asked her if I could return the flies if they didn't work. "If I buy a toaster and it doesn't work, I can return that, can't I?" I said. "Yeah, but it doesn't work like that around here, sonny boy," she said.

A handsome rainbow is this fisherman's reward.

I admitted to her my frustration with fishing the local waters. Well, of course she talked me into hiring one of her guides for the evening. How could I say no? At 3 p.m. I met fishing guide Chuck Paige at the Sunrise Fly Shop. Before we left, I had a quick ham sandwich at the Hitching Post, right next door. As I finished eating, I noticed the wind picking up, and by the time Chuck, Kristie, who was coming with us to shuttle the vehicles, and I left the shop, dark clouds were moving in and the wind was really rockin' and rollin'.

We drove about forty-five minutes into the middle of nowhere and maneuvered the raft onto the river. The landscape was dry, mountainous wilderness. It wasn't a place you wanted to be stranded. There were rattlesnakes, scrub pines, caves and dead things. I didn't like it there.

First it started to rain. Then the temperature dropped from about eighty-five to sixty degrees. The wind was blowing between thirty and forty miles per hour. It didn't look good. But we were here and storms usually blow over quickly in the mountains, so off we went.

Fishing in the wind is the ultimate challenge for fly fishermen, and forty-mile-per-hour winds are a nightmare, especially when the wind blows steadily in your face. The rubber raft we were in was blown sideways and turned around almost at will by the strong winds. My guide, Chuck, struggled with the raft and did the best he could. My first few casts were blown back in my face. No bugs could possibly fly in this wind, so the fishing was probably going to be off. But I had no choice. I was paying for this, so I had better make the best of it. I resigned myself to short casts.

But Chuck had a different approach. Like a true professional, he saw the day as full of opportunities.

The water was clear and no other fishermen were out. The fish could be hungry, since the wind had been blowing for a few days and the water was low.

Nonetheless, I was in for a bit of adjustment in terms of my approach to fly-fishing. Each guide in the world does things differently from the next, and each river is completely different from the next as well.

Chuck took my rod and rigged it with two dry flies. A large hopper was the end fly but attached about twenty inches below it was a tiny size-eighteen brown thing. Good enough, I thought. I had never fished like this before, but it looked good to me. We were not out there for small fish. Neither did we want whitefish. I wanted big Montana brown trout. I knew they were there. I had seen pictures of them; smiling fisherman holding big browns. I wanted one! Before I cast, however, I dressed in my waders and pulled on a warm fleece jacket over my raincoat. The wind and rain can kill you. Better to at least be comfortable, I thought.

The Big Hole fishes differently from any river I had fished. Usually, I'm a structure guy. I like throwing flies in deep pools, behind rocks, underneath trees and fallen logs, in shady areas, on deep-cut ledges — that's where the fish are so that's where I fish!

But the Big Hole is different. On certain days and at certain times of the year and when the weather is right, the big fish boldly hunt in shallow water and sit on shallow "beaches" or shelves. Today was one of those days. At Chuck's direction, I passed up tons of great-looking water. Frankly, I thought he was nuts and wondered if it was his first day on the job. But on my third cast to shallow water on a shallow edge — BAM! A twenty-inch brown hit my small dry fly. It wasn't a big hit, just a large mouth popping up out of the water and gulping my fly. I set the hook. The hook and line held. I played the fish well as Chuck struggled with the boat in fierce winds, then netted the fish. I was ecstatic. We made photos. I had proof!

Brown trout.

After we released the fish, we continued downstream. We had another hit, a good-looking fifteen-inch brown, then another. Next I landed a great-looking fourteen-inch rainbow that jumped all over the place. The big fish were in the shallows. I learned something new that day.

Monsters were not easy to catch. The big fish came gently and quickly out of nowhere and always hit the small fly. The action happens in milliseconds. Be prepared or you'll lose. I missed three big fish (above twenty-four inches). Everything has to be right to land monsters of that size. The hook set has to be perfect and the timing right. There are a million variables, the most important being getting the fish to hit in the first place and that means perfect casts and perfect equipment.

Fish are not stupid, as arrogant humans often perceive them to be. They have been on the planet for about sixty million years. They are marvels of creation and capable of standing up to extreme and ever-changing elements. They can swim for thousands of miles and return to the exact place where they were originally hatched. They know what they need to know in order to survive, so fish are always where they are supposed to be. They are never out of place. Their habitat is well defined. Know the fish and you'll catch them.

Chuck Paige was the ultimate professional. He checked my rig constantly, retied knots when necessary, trimmed the flies, dried them almost to excess, told me where to cast and often spotted the strike before I did. He also handled the boat well in very difficult circumstances. I caught twenty fish that day even though I had, because of the nasty elements, expected nothing. I was thrilled. I would do it again in a second. Surprisingly, I caught all my fish on the flies that Kristie had sold me. I would return to her store in a few days to thank her and to purchase more.

We got out of the water about nine that evening and had a pizza for dinner at the only pizza place in the town of Melrose. It was excellent!

That night I was a guest at the Big Hole Ranch, a private fishing club on the banks of the Big Hole River with only thirteen members. Nearly impossible to find, the ranch includes four log guest cabins and a meeting and eating lodge. The entire setting — the meals, the individual fly-tying desks in the lodge, the ambiance, the physical grounds, the personalities of the gracious hosts — was world class. My host, co-owner Bob Esperti, is a former member of the United States Fly Fishing Team and is the greatest fly fisherman I've ever met. It was great to be able to spend three days at the camp.

On the evening of my second day there, Bob got down to the basics of fly-fishing. After dinner he and I went to the tackle room to look at equipment. Whatever I had thought before, in the presence of a very experienced, knowledgeable professional who had spent more than forty years meticulously studying every aspect of the art of fly-fishing, I realized I was an absolute neophyte within the realm of fly-fishing.

During the next three hours he had me tying leaders and knots of all sorts. He was an exceptional teacher. In the past, I had been using nine-foot tapered leaders. All that changed when I learned that his leaders were more than twenty feet long. The butt of his leader was thirty pounds, connected to twenty-five-pound, twenty-pound, fifteen-pound and all the way down to four- and sometimes two-pound tippet material. Each section was carefully connected to the other by a perfectly tied blood knot. He also occasionally used up to five flies on his line, each connected to the leader. Extra flies were not connected to the end hook; rather, each was tied independently to the leader to insure strength and to minimize the possibilities of tangling.

We talked of hook sets, casting methods, fishing with Europeans on foreign rivers, equipment, flies and all kinds of stuff. I asked a thousand questions. He answered them all. At eleven that night, I wandered to my cabin and practiced a few knots before I passed out. I was a new man. It isn't often that people get to spend that much time with such a capable and willing teacher.

In the morning we met in front of the camp pond. Bob tied a mid-size Royal Wulf onto his twenty-foot leader. We wandered down to the pond, standing at least fifteen feet back from the edge of the water. He cast his fly and BAM! After a ten-minute battle, he landed a six-pound rainbow trout. I could hardly believe it. As I stood near the pond, I noticed monster ten-pound trout swimming like sharks and attacking anything that fell in the water.

My host had me throw the fly several times, graciously offering tips on casting. I watched with interest as trout the size of footballs eyed my flies. Later, I said my thanks and departed; duty called and I had miles to go, but I hoped I would return to the Big Hole Ranch someday. It was a perfect little slice of heaven.

I drove back to the Sunrise Fly Shop and chatted again with Kristie Piazzola. I had her pick out a dozen more flies for me that would no doubt sooner or later catch more great fish. While we talked, I looked at the photos on the walls, the flies, the tackle and the other gear. I checked my schedule and where I was supposed to be the following day.

As Lyle Lovett says, "What would you be if you didn't try? You have to try." So without further thought, I opened my mouth: "Any guides available today?" Within a few minutes, I had whipped out my charge card and was making plans to return to Big Hole. Chuck Paige, who had guided me a few days earlier, met me within a half hour and off we went back to the river.

Before he arrived I had a quick monster pancake breakfast next door at the Hitching Post. I remembered some of the same people who had been there a few days earlier, and the waitress remembered me. I was becoming a regular.

Of course, the wind picked up dramatically and the temperature dropped at least twenty degrees during our drive to the put-in. The skies were almost black. Once at the river, I pulled on all my clothes and prepared for the worst. I was not disappointed. First hail, then rain and then snow. The wind blew at a constant forty miles per hour. This was "fishing from hell" at its finest. The boat spun in all directions. My fly line suspended itself in midair, then came whipping back in my face. Huge trees swayed so extremely far over that we were scared to death that they would fall on us. It stayed that way for hours. It would not subside until an hour before the trip was over and we were in the slack, dead water.

But on my third cast I landed a gorgeous twenty-inch brown. It fought harder and had bigger shoulders than any of the fish I had caught a few days earlier. Once again, my guide demonstrated his ability to excel at his craft. We caught fish all day long. He did not fish, but as I cannot take pictures of myself fishing, Chuck graciously served as model with my fish.

We probably caught another twenty fish throughout the day, the largest just more than twenty inches. It was another cold but thrilling day. A few other fishermen out on boats commented that the fishing was slow to nonexistent. We had initially fished with brown hoppers with a tiny size-eighteen dry fly attached as a trailer, but as the day progressed, we switched to a Royal Wulf as the end fly and another tiny dry attached to that.

As we neared the pullout that evening, the skies finally cleared and the wind died. We said our good-byes and I made my way back to the Hitching Post for a spaghetti dinner. From there, I drove back to Bozeman, where I spent the night at a friend's house. There was no heat in the house. I nearly froze to death as the nighttime temperature dropped into the thirties.

Papoose Creek Lodge

I found my way to the Papoose Creek Lodge alongside the Madison River, about forty miles east of Ennis, Montana. The lodge is a very high-end setting that specializes in eco-tourism; they offer a variety of wilderness activities. Most people come to relax, take advantage of the stunning scenery and fish the Madison. The lodge is extraordinary, each cabin a piece of artwork in itself, the ambiance exceptional, the food out of this world and the hosts and guides professional and as courteous as can be.

Before dinner, cocktails were served and I met most of the other ten or so guests. Most had traveled great distances to get there. Dinner was served family-style but one could order from a number of entrées. Chef Bill Growning, an exceptional culinary artist, dazzled us with a variety of appetizers, entrées and desserts. Dinner was a two-hour affair.

I rose early in the morning, about five-thirty, wrote for a while on my laptop and then headed for the kitchen. As the other guests would not eat until eight or so, it was just me and the staff who came wandering in. The ranch manager, a few fishing guides and the horse guy (I don't know exactly what his title was, but he took care of the horses and oversaw the trail riding) — the "local color" — were all early risers. We had breakfast and I listened as they talked about the rodeo circuit, bull riding, bears, dances, their lives and other fascinating stuff. Anybody who does not take the time to hear the lives of others is missing one of the great adventures of being human.

I returned to my room reflecting on my early fly-fishing adventures. In the eighties I had lived in Massachusetts, where my neighbor was a fly fisherman who offered to take me out anytime. One Saturday I took him up on his offer. We went out in the evening and enjoyed a great number of hits on a small lake. He suggested that I get out of the boat and wade, so I did. I was wearing shorts and a pair of sneakers.

In time, I climbed back into the boat. To my absolute horror, more than twenty leeches had attached themselves to my legs. It was absolutely disgusting. My neighbor was laughing. I hated him. I demanded to be taken home immediately. Eventually, I had to burn off the leeches with lit

Papoose Creek Lodge is as comfy as home — but the meals are better than home.

matches. I never spoke with him again, and I didn't pick up a fishing pole for at least five years. Nor did I swim in any lakes. Many years later, the thought still disgusts me. Maybe I need therapy.

After breakfast I met my fishing guide for the day, Michael Henry, a seasoned veteran of the Montana fishing scene. We spent a good half hour talking about the local waters before we agreed on where to fish. Eventually, we decided on a small lake about an hour north of Ennis. The drive up was eventful. Herds of pronghorn antelope were visible from the road. Anglers were busy fishing from drift boats on the legendary Madison River beneath the big blue sky of Montana. We soon found the shores of the lake, put in the boat and ventured out.

The lake was like glass; not a ripple anywhere. A major *Callibaetis* hatch prevented one from breathing too deeply. Bugs were everywhere. We paddled slowly and quietly across the lake. We were hunters hunting fish – big ones – with extraordinary colors, strength and survival skills. They weren't stupid. They hated us and would do anything to avoid contact with the ones who hunted them. They knew we were after them. Just like they know when an osprey or eagle is overhead.

Like our ancestors of millions of generations ago, we felt the beating of our hearts and the pumping of our blood as we first observed and then approached them. Humans lived too long as hunter/gatherers for this moment to be ignored. We are all hunters, whether we like it or not.

Michael paddled slowly and deliberately. I sat low in the stern as we approached them. I was ready. The water was shallow, not deeper than four feet anywhere in the lake. I could see their fins and their mouths as they rose quietly from the depths, exerting almost no energy. They seemed to just gulp and suck in dormant and dead insects floating on the surface. They would come up for a few seconds and then be gone, keeping close to each other, always three or four rising at any one time.

I was using a number-twelve Royal Wulf – a deadly little insect. The fish were rising maybe twenty yards from our boat. I stripped line from my reel. I made a few false casts, first to get enough line out and second to insure that the fly was completely dry. I wanted a soft, flutter of a landing for the fly once I cast it. I wanted it to be as natural as possible.

I loaded up on the back cast. I let the line fly toward the trout. It landed three feet from the last swirl. There it sat like a ship on the ocean. Looking magnificent, it was a pure beacon of light on a river of glass. I held my breath. We didn't speak. The fish were coming closer and closer. Our hearts pounded. A mouth opened. The fly was gone. I lifted the rod. The hook was set. Terror set in the mind and heart of the fish. He fought like a survivor should. He ran and ran. He took my line to the backing. He jumped high three times. Eventually, he tired and was brought to the net. He was twenty inches. I removed the hook, photographed him and released him back to his home waters. He took his time about reviving but eventually darted from my hands. It was a good day.

Later, another hatch occurred. There was still absolutely no wind. Gorgeous tiny bugs covered our hands, vests and legs and went up our noses. It was like a snowstorm. With the bugs came more rising fish. We continued our hunt, quiet and stealthy. We knew what we were doing. The variables, hundreds of them, all came together.

Around two-thirty the wind came up and killed the fishing. Michael struggled to bring the boat back to shore. The clouds came in and knocked down the bugs; there would be no more fishing on this lake for the day. This type of fishing, however, remains close to my heart. The still water, the hunt, the cast, the rises, the hits, the fights and the runs thrill me. But equally important was the communication between fisherman and guide. We each knew what to do and I could not have caught fish without the experience and skill of my guide, Michael Henry. We caught about twelve fish that day. We missed several but missed fish are a blessing. God made fishing to keep strong men humble. Constant success becomes boredom. Challenges keep us young and alive.

On the way back to Papoose Creek Lodge, Michael suggested that we try a private section of the Madison River. How could I say no?

[THIS PAGE] *Guide Michael Henry takes a prized trout from the Big Hole.*

August 13

THE YELLOWSTONE RIVER

Wildlife
is evident
at almost
every
bend of
the river.

I spent the night in Columbus, Montana, in an

"el cheapo" motel just across the street from the railroad tracks. It was the only room left in town. Unfortunately the rooms adjacent to mine were booked with some serious bikers who partied until almost daybreak. They must have played "Born to Run" about a thousand times. Since I couldn't beat 'em I was tempted to join them, but I knew nothing of Harley carburetors and didn't think they would be interested in a conversation about the local stone fly hatch. At one point they commented on how noisy the train was as it passed through town. They finally fell asleep just as a rooster cock-a-doodle-dooed right outside my window.

The park was subject to a tremendous forest fire in the late eighties. A fly fisherman wades on the Madison River while dead snags stand sentinel as a reminder of the devastation caused by fires.

Despite my scanty sleep, I met my guide, Mike Mouat, at eight in the morning, then had a quick breakfast at a fast-food joint and was ready to go. One of four clients, I rode with the other guide, Steve, Mike's older brother. Both were legendary fishermen in the area and had fished the waters of the Yellowstone region for many years. I would be fishing with Mike and an older friend of his who had fished with him for years, a retired attorney. The trip up to the boat launch took almost an hour.

The Yellowstone River is different from other rivers in the area. Flowing south and then north out of Lake Yellowstone, it meanders casually through a region of both rolling hills and flat lands. Lined by an occasional group of towering cottonwoods, the river is surprisingly clear of fallen trees and other debris. Wildlife is evident at almost every bend of the river — deer, antelope, eagles and osprey are common sights.

This river isn't undiscovered. On a normal day in midsummer, there would be twenty or so boats, plus waders, fishing the river. But we were fortunate: ours were the only two boats that day.

The day started out badly for me. Besides having slept fitfully (or because of it), I forgot to bring my fishing vest that had all my flies, tools, tippet material and other stuff. But Mike was an understanding person. We kidded about getting older and the "forgetfulness" that was sneaking up on both of us. Fortunately, he had enough gear for just about everyone on the planet. The only other apparent problem was the wind. Blowing at a steady twenty miles per hour, it would hinder us through most of the day.

As there were billions of grasshoppers on the fields surrounding the river, we used hopper patterns with a Copper John as a drop nymph behind the end fly. For the first hour we caught only a few very small trout. Little nymphs attract little fish. But in the second hour I landed an eighteen-inch rainbow with big shoulders. It took the hopper. We made the obligatory photos and released it. Just as I had another great hit — the fish was clearly hooked — my cell phone rang. Now, I love my wife and hadn't spoken with her for three days, but while I fumbled with the phone, I lost the fish. That will never happen again.

Halfway through the trip an incident happened that could have been catastrophic. The river is a classical swift float with occasional class-two and -three rapids. The water was fairly clear with a very light green stain to it. Mike, a lifelong rafter with very significant experience in all kinds of water, knew what he was doing and I had confidence in him. Midday we entered a set of class-two rapids. At face value it was not a big deal. I had taught whitewater canoeing for many years and only gave the rapids a second glance. I continued fishing without even questioning Mike's ability to ease us through the rapids.

[THIS PAGE] *Every once in a while a fish comes up. To the surprise of everyone, I caught this impressive trout on a dry fly on the Madison River just inside the park.*
[OPPOSITE] *Sunshine Creek is a small stream flowing out of the east side of Yellowstone National Park. Guide Andy Fisher executes a short cast to entice one of the many brook trout that inhabit the stream.*

We were traveling sideways through the rapids when the downstream oar hit a rock and shot upwards. Mike held on but was pulled up to a standing position. Suddenly we dropped over another rock and the raft bent in half. Mike was pulled violently into the water. It was several hair-raising seconds before he came to the surface. This was not a laughing matter. Being downstream of the boat, he could have easily been pinned against a rock. I rose from my seat and fumbled with the remaining oar. After several seconds I was able to spin the raft around and got him on the upstream side of the boat. All he had to do now was hang on. But the water was deep and it took longer than I hoped to pass through the rapids and steer the boat to shore.

Finally, the water calmed out and Mike scrambled back into the boat. Eventually we also retrieved the oar and his hat and continued on.

The lesson for me was that even the most experienced professional can run into trouble. It took just a millisecond for him to be in the water. It was also a reminder that everyone, guides included, should always wear a life preserver.

Within a few minutes of Mike climbing back into the boat, we reorganized ourselves and were fishing again. It was windy and hot and very dry due to the drought, so Mike dried out quickly and we all had a good, if nervous, laugh about it.

All in all, however, we enjoyed ourselves. At the end of the day, each of us had caught a few good-size fish and a number of small fellows. Mike took great pains to fish some almost inaccessible waters because of the wind. As the wind blew in our faces most of the day, he handled the boat and the mediocre fishing as well as possible. I would fish with him again in an instant.

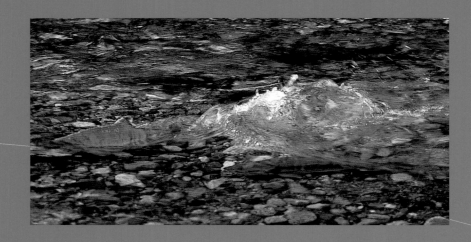

August 18

KING PACIFIC LODGE

The whole system is contingent on the return of the salmon.

Guide Ken Beatty and a young
guest stand waist deep in the cold
waters to retrieve their catch.

I reluctantly left Montana. It had been a great
five weeks. But the time had come to go home to my wife and daughter, my
business and reality. Not that I didn't want to stay — far be it from me to
avoid responsibilities and play the rest of my life — but necessity calls.

Michele and Lindsey picked me up in Albany around 11 p.m. and we had a great ride home. I finally fell asleep around three in the morning.

At 7 a.m. Lindsey woke me with "Morning time, Daddy! Will you make me pancakes, please?" How could I say no?

Around 10 a.m. I looked at my calendar and to my horror realized that on that today I was to leave for the King Pacific Lodge in the Queen Charlotte Islands, off the coast of British Columbia. Most people would be thrilled to be going to a place like this, but I was tired of traveling, airports, fast food and running around. I wanted to sleep in my own bed in my own house and be with my family.

With full realization that I was to leave within two hours, I unpacked my bags from Montana and repacked them for the Queen Charlotte Islands. Michele drove me to the airport. We said our good-byes and I reluctantly departed. I was fortunate to not get a lecture from her.

The plane, a very small ten-passenger, first took me to Toronto. There I had to reclaim my luggage, go through customs, explain why I had scissors, hooks, knives and other such stuff in my luggage, and then repack and lug my gear to a terminal that I am certain was miles away.

Finally, after much effort, I found the gate. It was to be a full flight. We waited and waited. The plane was broken and they were looking for a new plane to take us to Vancouver. Two hours and several hot dogs later, they were finally ready to board. Then the weather turned bad and the airplanes on the runway began to line up and then back up. Three hours later we finally took off. It was a six-hour flight. My body ached. I wanted to stretch my legs. I was near a point where I could have turned around and gone home.

However, we finally arrived in Vancouver, where it took an hour for the luggage to show up at the baggage station. Then I had to fill out several forms, go through customs, find a cart and find the airport hotel. It took almost two additional hours to get to the registration desk and to my room.

Once I was relaxing in bed, around midnight, someone tried to get into my room. They were assigned the same room as I. They returned to the front desk. An hour later another knock on the door. It was the manager apologizing for the misunderstanding. He presented me with two bottles of beer and hot pretzels. What could I say? I finally fell asleep at 4 a.m.

I awoke an hour and a half later and met the travel host and the other lodge guests in the lobby. After breakfast we departed for customs and more forms, but as I was about to board the plane, I noticed that none of my luggage had been checked. The hotel forgot to have my bags brought to the terminal. The plane was held while the guide, Ronne Ludvigson, sent someone to my room for my gear — another half hour wasted. My blood pressure was definitely up. I wanted to be home with my family.

Once we arrived in Prince Rupert, we had to wait another hour for a bus to take us to the docks for the pontoons. We also had to carry our own luggage. As I had bags of photo gear, computers, and fishing equipment, mine was excessively heavy — more than a hundred pounds. Once at the dock, I was told that I couldn't have more than thirty pounds of luggage. Some of it could not come. Frankly, I'd had it. I was ready to go home.

But a solution was found and my extra stuff was brought out on another flight. I boarded a small Beaver pontoon and took off with the other guests. The flight to Princess Royal Island and the King Pacific Lodge was spectacular.

King Pacific Lodge —
first-class accommodations
for folks experiencing world-
class scenery.

Five minutes after we landed, my attitude turned around 180 degrees. The hotel staff was extraordinarily friendly, the lodge, stunning and the scenery, out of this world. Calmness prevailed. Reason returned. It was good to be there. I was okay again.

First lunch: very high end, gourmet everything. The Canadian staff was wonderful and everything was professional. The other guests, an international crowd, were great; we talked about all kinds of stuff.

My first fishing venture was off a boat. I was paired with guide Carlin Bennett and another fly fisherman. Off we went across the bay, where we would be fishing for pink salmon in an isolated cove. The fish were staging in shallow waters before entering a stream for spawning. As we entered, cove plums of mist exploded from the surface. Humpback whales were blowing air underwater and feeding on the fish that found themselves caught in the fray. Then three curious sea lions entered the scene and entertained us for several minutes with their antics. Eagles were everywhere above us. We were really close. It was a magical sight.

I landed a pink salmon on every other cast and had a hit on just about every cast. The flies were small chartreuse streamers with barbless hooks and I was using a five-weight rod. The guides strongly encouraged me to use heavier gear — one of the house nine-weights. But I know how to use my gear. It's not necessary to muscle in a fish. If the drag is set properly, you can land just about any size fish on light tackle. Just let the drag and the rod do what they were designed to do.

Father and son team Henry and François Moser from Switzerland display their catch along the Green River. Notice who has the larger fish.

One right after the other, the fish hit my line. Schools of fish surfaced all over. The guide professionally maneuvered the boat so that we had access to the fish. It was a great afternoon. I was calming down. We returned to the lodge around four and I took an extended nap.

Dinner was at seven. I sat with other guests, including two gentlemen from Switzerland, Henry and François. The conversation was lively, the food was excellent and the service was commendable. I retired for the evening a content man.

AUGUST 20 As I write this, I'm still shaking. I'm not kidding. I am certain I'll lose sleep over the experience. It's now evening and I recall, in vivid detail, the extraordinary events of the day.

I had a quick breakfast at around 6 a.m. I was going fishing with Henry and François. Our host was Ken Beatty, an experienced man with a long résumé of wilderness guiding. Out on the dock, the wilderness silence was broken. The noise got louder and louder; a helicopter was landing. "Get in," the guide said. I did. We were off to the Green River somewhere in the interior of British Columbia. There are thousands of rivers in this area that have never been fished. It is, without a doubt, an absolute paradise for fisherman. The ride to the interior was stunning, the scenery was almost unreal. We flew over mountains that hosted thousand-foot cliffs. Beautiful mature forests surrounded the clear blue waters of lakes and rivers. There were no roads, no telephone poles, no radio towers, no fast-food stations and no footprints. There was just absolutely pristine wilderness. I fully expected Big Foot to pop out from around any corner. But what I got was worse.

The flight was mostly uneventful. I was strapped into a window seat in the rear of the aircraft. Suddenly and without warning, when we were at least a few thousand feet in the air, my door swung open! I can assure you that this was not a good thing. I was looking straight down thousands of feet into coastal rainforest. The pilot calmly told me to reach out, grab the door and shut it. So with fear in my heart, I leaned way out of the chopper, grabbed the door and pulled. The latch would not work. I had to sit and hold the door closed for the duration of the flight. I can assure you it was more than a bit unnerving.

As we landed in the absolute middle of nowhere, two monster grizzly bears ran from the noise of the chopper. Okay, they are gone, I thought. Good. Thank God.

We were on the shores of the extraordinary Green River, as serene as any place could be. Thousands of spawning chum salmon were upstream and downstream, there for the taking. Huge, explosive and fascinating, they followed the call to return to their home waters to procreate and die.

In truth, it was not a pretty site. One felt a bit of sorrow for these creatures who would never see their children or return to the open sea that had been their home for years. They would become hideously deformed and die within a short time, their bodies rotting in the sun or on the bottom of clear waters. They would never be remembered by their offspring. They would be gone forever.

But new life springs from their personal tragedies. Other creatures, eagles, gulls, bears, and microbes of all sorts, would benefit from their deaths and life would go on. It's a strange tale, but it's the formula of the world we endure. Life goes on.

Every inch of the ground we were walking on was covered with bear tracks — and I mean big bear tracks. We were actually keeping these big bears from their lunch and the more I thought about it, the more I realized this was not a good thing. In Alaska, bears generally avoid people. In Alaska, humans hunt them or watch them from platforms feeding on rivers and streams. Many Alaskan bears are completely comfortable around people. They only want fish, not people.

But the bears here had probably never seen humans. They only knew that we were on their property and preventing them from eating. Ken assured us that the bears would be no problem, so we went about the business of fishing. Not long later, I saw a huge bear chasing salmon a few blocks upstream. He is incredibly fast, I thought to myself. But as no one else saw him as he disappeared around a corner, I put him completely out of my mind. I made the very conscious effort to trust our guide and ignore the bears and resolved myself to enjoying the day.

The two other guests hadn't fly-fished before, so Ken masterfully coached them to near-perfect casting throughout the day. The fishermen became competent very quickly.

I found a small pool and began casting for pinkies. I did not have to wait long. With my first and second casts, I landed strikes and fish. This went on all day; just about every cast hit a fish. I did not always land them, but the fishing was nonstop. Considering that we were using barbless hooks, it was surprising that we did not lose more of them. But if we kept the proper tension on the line, we could land as many as we wanted. After each fish was caught, it was promptly released back to the water. Catch and release is the law in these parts.

Late in the morning I heard a "woof woof" sound quite a ways away. It was clearly the aggressive sound a bear makes when he is agitated. Then I heard it again. More "woofs" and louder this time. It was getting closer and closer. I mentioned it to Ken, who seemed completely unconcerned. I could hear the sound of crashing trees. It was near.

Then he appeared on the beach just upstream from us. He was huge, the biggest bear I have ever seen. He first caught a salmon and fed on it. Then he eyed me. I told Ken, but he couldn't see the bear even though I pointed it out to him. And it was coming toward us. I assured Ken that the bear was real, and for the life of me, I could not understand why he didn't see the thing. Finally, after once again pointing out the advancing bear, Ken saw it. It was a huge, angry, hungry, mature male grizzly. And he was coming directly toward us!

Once Ken saw the bruin, he stopped what he was doing and said, "We should get out of here now." There was a dire sense of urgency in his voice. We picked up our bags and left. We didn't run. We just very quickly picked up our gear and left that fishing hole.

So we moved downstream a hundred yards or so and found another great fishing hole, its banks lined with five-hundred-year-old trees. Not a footprint, cigarette butt, candy wrapper or beer can was to be found. These are pristine, virgin forests. I sincerely hoped that we humans have the foresight and ability to preserve these lands. It would be immoral if we didn't.

The fishing continued to be excellent and I fair-hooked three huge chum salmon. Our guide landed a great twelve-pound silver salmon, and I continued to land pinks one right after the other. Near the end of the day I foolishly tried to remove a fly from a very active salmon. Unfortunately, the fish jumped at the wrong time and I succeeded in burying a hook deep in my hand — barb and all. The hook had gone in and was partially exposed through a second hole. It hurt like hell and was a bloody mess. Fortunately, I had removed many hooks from other people, so I knew what to do: keep my hand in the stream for several minutes so the cold water could numb it. I tried to push the hook completely through, but it was too painful. Finally, I depressed the hook and painfully backed it out the same way it had come in. As I write this, my hand is sore and swollen, but I didn't let it ruin my day.

I know that in truth, bears pose little threat to humans as long as you don't do something stupid, don't run and don't show fear. I also know that guides are perfectly capable of dealing with such problems.

I admit I have a paranoid side of my personality and probably a tendency to dwell a bit too much on some things. I'm certain that I have an obsessive-compulsive side to me. Come to think of it, I probably have a ton of things about myself that I wish I could change. But no one is ever perfect and we all come with excess baggage. You do the best you can and you work on the things you don't necessarily like about yourself.

But the bears profoundly impacted my day. They scared me. Every inch of the river was covered with bear tracks. And it probably did me no good to have read every book ever written about bear attacks before I came to the lodge. (I've also read just about everything written about shark attacks. And I do not swim in the ocean — period.)

So what in the world was I doing in Bear City?

Finally, the helicopter arrived. We were going home. Once we were onboard and cruising over the mainland, the pilot told us that he would have been there sooner, but the chopper had broken down and wouldn't start. "It's okay now, though," he said as we cruised over jagged mountains. I was happy to hear the craft was airworthy. I kept my eyes shut for most of the ride back to the lodge!

Dinner was at seven-fresh, hot, gourmet food, delicious and exquisite in every detail. I sat around a roaring fire pit on the dock with a group of other guests and we talked until nearly midnight. The stars were brilliant and the air was cool. In contrast to the day I had just experienced, it was one of the most relaxing evenings I've ever spent.

The morning brought a few clouds but perfectly calm water. It was low tide and the aroma of the sea was everywhere. Out my window, just yards away, salmon leaped for the joy of it. Eagles eyed them from overhead.

Around nine in the morning, I motored off in a boat with guide Ronne Ludvigson. We traveled about ten minutes to a tiny section called Taylor Bight. Deciding to have some fun with the salmon, I rigged up a seven-foot three-weight, put ten-pound tippet material on the leader and finished the rig out with a small pink streamer.

Huge schools of salmon swam beneath the boat. Thousands finned and rolled in the small cove, just waiting for more rain and high tide before they began the journey upstream that would ultimately cost them their lives. Huge trees lined the shores. Eagles carefully eyed the schools. Ravens called from the interior of the woods, just out of eyesight. Below us, huge sunflower starfish moved on the rocks, unmindful of time. Enormous kelp beds swayed to the rhythm of the currents. Bears would no doubt soon be here to put on extra pounds for the winter. The whole system is contingent on the return of the salmon.

One by one, the salmon hit my line. These were fair-caught fish. I only foul-hooked one the entire day. The three-weight bent like limp hair in the wind, but the line and knots held. I took my time about landing them; there was no hurry. Each fish took between ten and twenty minutes.

Finally, as expected, my tippet broke from the weight of an aggressive salmon. But just for the challenge and the fun, I decided to push the envelope. I tied a four-pound tippet onto my leader, then another small pink streamer, and I got a hit on the first cast. I set the drag on almost minimum. The fish took line. These salmon were in the three- to ten-pound range. They were fresh from the sea. Strong, tough and courageous, they ran and jumped like rodeo broncos. My line held, although it took just about forever to land them.

Early in the day the author buried this salmon fly deep in my hand. (Removing it was a painful, bloody mess!) Later, the salmon below swallowed the fly and graciously fed four hungry fishermen.
[OPPOSITE] The author battles, and successfully landed, a large pink salmon on a three-weight rod with four-pound tippet!

For the three hours we fished the bight with fish on just about every cast. No need to muscle them, there was plenty of time. We released each back to their world with a thank-you and a wish for the best.

I was surprised at how picky they were. Just for fun, I tried several different salmon flies that I've successfully used in Alaska. I tried orange, red, black, chartreuse, green and other-colored wet flies as well, to no avail. The salmon here wouldn't eat anything other than the small pink streamers that were hand-tied each evening by the guides. Maybe that's why they're called pink salmon.

We returned to the lodge but not before checking out the sea lions and some of the scenery. Throughout the day, I felt awed by the fact that there were no other fishermen, no hordes of boats, no jet planes or jet boats or trucks or billboards. There was only wilderness — just as the world was meant to be.

That evening we had another great dinner of king salmon and duck. The dinner lasted almost two hours. It was nine-thirty before I went to my room. In general — and I am convinced of this — what makes a place really great isn't only the staff but also the guests. I've stayed in high-end places all over North America and if the staff remains distant and the other guests are, shall we say, "stuffy," then the entire stay is a lesser experience.

On the other hand are really great places like the King Pacific Lodge whose staff was consistently friendly. On many occasions we invited them to join us for cocktails and evening conversation, and we found that they joined right in and were an integral part of the week we spent there. Further, the other guests at the lodge were fascinating. Our conversations lasted for hours, and I found that I had to excuse myself late at night to finally catch up on some sleep.

AUGUST 22 I was up at about 4 a.m. I had gone to bed early, around 10 p.m. I generally sleep for six hours total. Any six hours will do. So I typed on my laptop for a while, then read a book on shark attacks that happened in 1916 on the New Jersey shore. Then I fell asleep around six and had nightmares.

At 7:30 a.m. we had homemade waffles with butter and strawberries, fresh orange juice and coffee for breakfast. I passed on the bacon, ham, sausage, croissants, coffee rolls, gourmet teas, seven-grain bread, juices, fresh-cut fruit, gourmet cereal and a ton of other stuff. My guide, Ronne, and I left the dock at just after eight. It was cool, foggy and raining and a breeze was just starting to blow. After a twenty-minute ride, we set up the boat with down riggers. We also rigged up a buck-tail streamer for my eight-weight fly rod that was to be trolled behind the boat. We were fishing for cohos — big ones. Several had been taken during the last few days, so we had decided to try our luck. We lowered our lines.

Unfortunately, an hour later, no boats in the area, including ours, had a hookup. We broke down the gear and moved westward toward a kelp bed known for holding huge sea bass that would strike flies. We didn't make it that far. A strong breeze picked up and the waves battled our small boat. We decided to turn around. Eventually, with the help of a sophisticated GPS, we found our way back to Taylor Bight. It was in a safe harbor where the water was calm. The fog now had covered everything and it was a chore to see the shores of the many islands we passed.

Once we arrived at the bight, I decided to see how extreme I could go. Onto my three-weight rod I placed a very tiny fly reel and tied on two-pound test line as tippet material. I lost my first three fish, though it wasn't my fault; they kept tangling themselves in kelp beds, which resulted in broken lines.

But soon I got the hang of it. Without giving them any play, I simply dragged them out of the weed beds into open water. There they could pull all they wanted. I am happy to report that I succeeded in landing several eight-pound fish. It's just a matter of timing. There is no need to pull on these fish. It's just letting them tire themselves out, getting them to the boat and then releasing the hook (which, by the way, was barbless!).

Later, I ate too much for lunch — great French onion soup, salmon with stuff on top and monstrous chocolate cookies for desert. I wanted to take a nap afterwards but was talked into going out again with a guide and an inexperienced fisherman. We returned, in the rain, to Taylor Bight. It was now high tide and fish were beginning to enter the river, but new schools of fish were also just arriving from their odyssey in the sea. Huge schools of pink salmon glided and finned their way toward the stream. The water churned and swirled with fish. At any given time, at least four could be seen leaping out of the water.

I rigged my eight-weight. My hands were cold and wet. The rain kept rolling into my eyes, making the tying of knots difficult. I made my first cast and got a hit right away. I handed the rod to the other guest on the boat. She had never caught a fish before and was thrilled. She landed it perfectly. She giggled and laughed through her first experience of fishing. Although a mature adult, she regressed to a four-year-old at play, loving every second of it! She was now permanently and forever addicted to fly-fishing. I let her land my fish the rest of the day. I hope she doesn't think that fishing is like that all the time. I assured her that she may never again have fishing this good. She just smiled.

Eventually, we were soaked to the bone and returned to the lodge through the fog and rain. Dinner was another extraordinary feast. I had the lamb. The King Pacific Lodge is well worth the price of admission.

Ronne Ludvigson enjoys playing a huge salmon.

AUGUST 23 It was my last day. The novice fisherman that I took out the evening before last had told everyone about her extraordinary afternoon. She came back and asked if I would take her and her friend out again in the morning. Our plane was to leave at 11 a.m., so I had to pack all my gear early. I acquiesced and agreed to take the two of them fishing. Actually, they just wanted the thrill of reeling in a fish. I would be happy to do it. I fully understand the thrill a guide gets when his first-time fishing clients catch fish. It's well worth the effort!

Unfortunately, the weather for the day was horrible. It had rained throughout the night and a major fog had settled over the area making visibility nonexistent. Nonetheless, four of us hopped into a boat and traveled back to the area where we had seen thousands of pinkies just the day before. Once there, we were disappointed to find that the river had risen and the tide was now high enough for thousands of salmon to enter the stream to begin the final episode of their lives. Not a single salmon was visible anywhere. They had gone home.

We ventured back to the lodge to begin our departure process. We could only travel a few miles per hour and because of the heavy fog we had to use the GPS to find the way. The planes were to leave at eleven o'clock.

Eventually, we returned to the lodge and brought our luggage down onto the docks for loading onto the planes that would soon be arriving.

On the radio we heard that the four planes had departed and were coming to take us first to Prince Rupert Island, then to Vancouver. We waited and waited in the thick fog. Finally, nearly two hours late, one of the planes landed. It could seat eight passengers. No one had heard from the other three planes in hours. Seven people got on. They had room for only one more. I was chosen; the others would have to stay.

Thankfully, the pilot was an experienced veteran of this area of the coast. He knew every island, inlet and passage. Because the fog was so thick, he could only taxi along the water. He could not fly. So for more than an hour, we traveled at about thirty miles per hour along the water. He was able to bring the plane above the water and fly at an altitude of about twenty feet. Fully aware that these passageways were used by major passenger ships, we all felt concern about slamming into a large vessel.

Eventually we landed on Prince Rupert Island. Five of the eight of us took off on a private jet; the other two and I had a pleasant visit and dinner on the island. I found my way back to Vancouver and then to Albany and finally, my home in the Adirondacks. Days later, as I give thought to the experience of the King Pacific Lodge, I find that I miss the camaraderie and professionalism of the facility. I realized again that people are the heart and soul of any experience. This wasn't just another high-end, five-star lodge or an expensive spa but a finely tuned home away from home that I keep thinking about over and over. I hope to return someday. I miss the place.

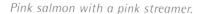
Pink salmon with a pink streamer.

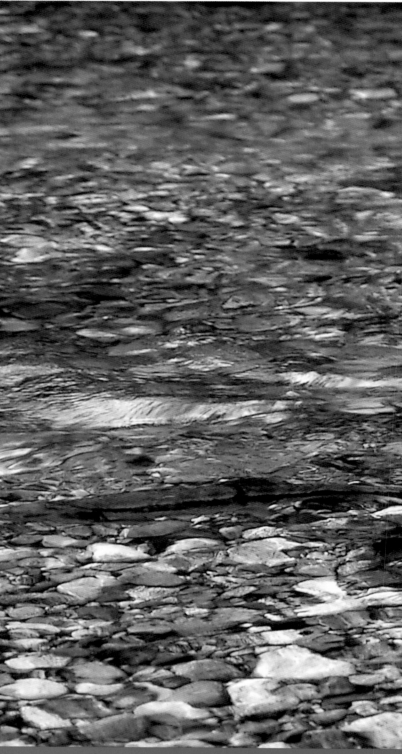

[THIS PAGE]   *Pink salmon is the catch of the day around Prince Rupert Island.*
[OPPOSITE]   *Spawning chum salmon.*

Fishermen display a proud catch and release a silver back to cold Canadian waters.

A happy guide from King
Pacific Lodge poses with a
large pink salmon.

August 30

BACK TO ALASKA

Sometimes
you're the
fire hydrant
and sometimes
you're
the dog.

Humans are pack animals. We group together. We conform.

We follow trends. We do things that will allow us to be accepted by others. As I sat in the airport in Dillingham, Alaska, waiting for my plane to take me fishing, I noticed the clothes and general appearance of the men in the waiting room. Most had some form of camouflage garment on. Everyone wore a baseball hat inscribed with a logo of some sort, whose sole purpose was to inform those looking at them where they had been or what brand of chewing tobacco they used or their favorite sports team. But hat logos, like logos of all sorts, are as much a statement about the individual as they are an advertisement about a product or service. Hats help to define personalities. If I see someone wearing a hat with a tobacco advertisement then I will have a predetermined idea about him or her.

Flowing toward the ocean and through the fishing village of Cordova, Alaska, the Eyak River is the site of a major salmon run. Picturesque vacation homes line the river and offer a perfect setting for warm-weather fishing.

People who wear similar "lifestyle" hats congregate together. I couldn't help but notice that six men, who I doubted knew each other before our extended wait in the airport lobby, seemed to be drawn together toward one corner of the room. Each wore a hat advertising NASCAR.

But one thing that characterized every man in the room, except myself, was that each had facial hair of some sort. Facial hair, in the world of outdoor sports, is a statement of ruggedness. It's a statement of manliness. Real men have facial hair.

As a product of the '60s, I had worn a mustache for many years. I thought it looked good and it was no doubt an attempt to conform to the styles of the day. But as I sat in the lobby of this airport with perhaps a hundred other men, each with their own style of facial hair, I thought about why I had shaved off my mustache years earlier.

I was a lecturer at Tufts University just outside of Boston. One day, one of my students approached me after class. She was extremely good looking and had caught the eye of every man on campus. When she smiled her blue eyes could melt any man. "Dr. Kylloe," she said, "you would look so much more handsome and younger if you just shaved off your mustache."

Within ten minutes of the class being over I had shaved off all my facial hair. I would never again attempt a beard or mustache. Women will never know the power they have over men. So be it!

But men have other traditions and conventions as well. No man in the world would ever ask another man to go into a bathroom with him. Women do this all the time. But men never do. Men never talk to each other in the toilet as well. It's strictly taboo. And real men never use the small urinal. That's for kids and small people. It's something all men understand. I've stood in line and

watched waiting until a full-size urinal became available. Also, if possible, guys will never stand next to each other and use a urinal. It just doesn't happen. It's a guy thing.

So they finally called out the various flights to the different wilderness lodges. One at a time, the men boarded their planes and went off to do battle with the elements. Each had his own reason for going and each would hopefully experience Alaska in a way that would increase the quality of his life. None of the men will probably ever know that I've made generalizations about them — us — but they provided me with four hours of entertainment and lessons. Now, as I board a 1950s pontoon, I just hope the fish are biting!

Back to Alaska

AUGUST 30 I'm very happy to be home. My bed is the most comfortable bed in the world. I read stories to my three-year-old daughter and relax with my wife there. It's a place where I feel safe and warm. My two cats come to me every evening, jump up and insist on being petted. After a ten-minute kitty massage, they jump down and sleep in their own beds.

It's Wednesday morning and I'm up early. I fed the cats, took a shower, responded to innumerable e-mail messages and started to pack. I brought out the warm stuff. It's cold in Alaska, and wet. I dug out my huge salmon flies, broke out my eight-weight rods and searched for my fishing gloves. I stuffed a down sleeping bag into the bottom of my duffel bag. Lodge owners are notorious for telling clients that their tents and cabins are heated. I wouldn't freeze in the night again. The sleeping bag always comes with me in the cool months.

[OPPOSITE] *The Eyak River receives little pressure from the fishing world because of its remote location. Nonetheless, when the fish are in, locals find time to cast a few flies to put meat on the table.*
[THIS PAGE-LEFT]
A first-time fly fisherman to the Alaskan waters, Dick Gil proudly shows off his largest fish ever on a fly rod! Fishing on the Eyak River has to be timed perfectly, as the bears come out at exactly 7 p.m. every evening to feast on salmon!
[THIS PAGE-RIGHT] *A young fisherman with his first salmon on the Eyak River.*

[THIS PAGE] *Guide Luke Conner "high-sticks" a salmon taken on the Tsiu River on Alaska's Lost Coast. Silver salmon are notorious for exploding at any second and breaking the rods of inexperienced fly fishermen. (I know because over the years I've broken four rods landing them.)*
[OPPOSITE-TOP] *Luke Conner proudly shows off a silver salmon I caught!*
[OPPOSITE-SECOND FROM TOP] *The hooked jaw of a silver salmon is indicative of a fish in the final stages of its life.*
[OPPOSITE-THIRD FROM TOP] *George Hayashida happily hugs a silver taken on a dry fly.*
[OPPOSITE-BOTTOM] *Luke Conner shows off a fresh-caught salmon. On some days one can actually feel the heat of the sun thus requiring the removal of several layers of clothing.*

The flight was supposed to leave Albany at 3 p.m. Michele and Lindsey drove me to the airport. I don't like saying good-bye again. A week earlier I offered to take them with me, but the trip would not be "child friendly." My daughter asked if she could watch *Sponge Bob* in Alaska. "No, Lindsey," I said. "They don't have TV where I'm going." They both decided to stay home.

I found my seat on the plane after being frisked and searched by a security guard who couldn't speak English. He didn't like the three old fish flies stuck in my hat that had sentimental meaning. He confiscated the hooks. I did not argue.

The flight was full. I got an isle seat. Moments later, a two-hundred-pound woman asks to slide into the window seat — no problem. Like a gentleman, I stood and helped her to stow her stuff in the overhead compartment. My mother would be proud. Then her three-hundred-pound husband showed up. He occupied the center seat. He is far too big to have the armrest down. The two of them take up the entire section. The flight attendant told me to sit down. "Where?" I asked. "In your seat, please." I hated her. I slide into my assigned seat. I might as well have sat on the gentleman's lap. I found that if I sat on my side and leaned out toward the isle, I could at least breathe. I needed to fasten my safety belt, but the only way I could do it was to sit flat in the seat. The man's arms were in my lap. I was being smothered. What could I do? There were no other seats on the plane.

The first thing he said to me was, "These seats are getting smaller and smaller each trip we make." I agreed with him. Then he complained about the heat. His sweat started to run down my arms. He complained to the flight attendant about the chairs, the lights, the late departure, the legroom and the magazines. With each statement, he got louder and louder. He was sweating like Niagara Falls. I prayed I would not have to do CPR on him.

Then he complained because they had no olives for a martini. Instead, he ordered four small bottles of Canadian Club. He drank them straight. His wife requested two bottles of Chardonnay. Then he asked for two box lunches instead of one, another two bottles of Canadian Club and more pretzels. His laughter shook the entire plane. My shirt and pants were soaked with his sweat. It was a bumpy ride, so we had to stay seated with our seat belts fastened. Near the end of the flight, we were offered coffee. "I'll have mine with Sweet'N Low," he said. He looked me right in the eye and winked. "We're watching our weight," he said. He and his wife break into riotous laughter. I could do nothing less than laugh with them. Sometimes in life you have to go with the flow. You can either be miserable or look for the humor in things that you can't control.

We finally landed in Chicago. My flight to Anchorage was delayed. I went to Bergdorfs in the airport terminal and ordered a corned beef sandwich and a beer. To my horror, the fat man and his wife sat next to me. He ordered four martinis for himself. We began talking. He bought me a beer. He downed his martinis like a toilet swallows dead goldfish. He was so loud that no one else in the restaurant was talking. He must have been a politician. Finally, I pried myself away from him and his wife. I thanked him for the beer. He leaned close and felt my wet shirt. "Spill something on you?" he asked. I didn't have the heart to tell him that my damp shirt was his sweat from our last flight. We finally said our farewells. Actually, I liked the couple. Their laughter was infectious and he certainly provided something for me to write about. Characters like him and his wife make life far more interesting.

The flight to Anchorage was late taking off. First it was one, then three, then five hours late. They found us a new plane. Everyone picked up their luggage and walked the half mile through the catacombs of the airport to the new plane. We didn't take off until 11 p.m. The gods had blessed me, however, by the three-seat section I had all to myself. I stretched out and slept during most of the seven-hour flight to Anchorage. It wasn't good sleep, but it was better than sitting upright in an airplane chair for several hours.

We finally arrived in Anchorage around 2 p.m. Anchorage time. I didn't know where I was. I found a cheap room in town for $165. No breakfast was included, but a free ride to and from the airport was. I fell asleep around 3 a.m. At 5 a.m. the phone rang with my wake-up call. I was back at the airport at 6 a.m. I grabbed a bagel and orange juice for $6.95.

The flight to Cordova, Alaska, left at 7:30 a.m. It was on time. Twenty minutes into the flight, the pilot got on the horn and told us that we were having an emergency. Fuel was not getting to the engines, he said. We did a 180-degree turn back toward Anchorage. The plane shook and rattled. I was scared to death. It was serious.

We finally landed in Anchorage amidst emergency trucks. Everything was okay. A new plane was wheeled out. We repacked our stuff, settled in and took off. An hour later, we landed in Cordova. It was raining. I rented a vehicle, a 1986 Caravan — was the only vehicle in town — at $70 a day.

Finally, I arrived at the Orca Adventure Lodge. It was a great place. I was thrilled to be there. We went fishing in the evening. Everyone on the river had reached their limits. The guide in my boat even caught his limit of three silvers in a day. I had no hits. I caught nothing. I ate dinner at the lodge, went to bed and slept for ten hours.

The following day I met a number of other guests, had a few great meals and enjoyed having the morning off. Around 3 p.m. I was introduced to Dick Gil, an amicable gentleman with considerable fly-fishing experience. It was his first day in Alaska. We agreed to go throw a few flies. An hour later, we wound up on the weir of the Eyak River. We rigged our gear and followed a trail. The silvers were in two places. They were holding just below the dam. And they were sitting in foot-deep water in the reeds on the edge of the lake. We started fishing. It was slow at first. Then Dick tied into a great salmon that kept him occupied for fifteen minutes. He was like a moose during the rut! Smiling from ear to ear, he finally landed his salmon. "I've been waiting twenty-four years for this," he said. I knew exactly how he felt and I was thrilled for him.

At six-thirty I mentioned that "during the days the water belongs to the humans, but at night the water belongs to the bears." I went on to say that at 7 p.m. the bears come out. He understood. At exactly 6:50 p.m. we packed up our gear and departed for the car. At exactly 7 p.m. we were in the vehicle. No more than fifteen seconds later, a huge black bear comes out of the woods, walks right in front of our vehicle and wanders down to the fishing hole.

"You weren't kidding about 7 p.m.," Dick said. No, I wasn't. We drove back to the lodge.

Silver salmon are perhaps the most extraordinary of the fighting fishes. When they are in and hitting, there is nothing like it. I've stood for hours in one spot and caught dozens of them, one right after the other. At face value, they are picky hitters. Humans, being a creative lot, have devised all sorts of academic approaches to catching them. Arguments range from surface flies like hot lips and poppers to wet flies such as spankers, egg-sucking leeches, Coho salmon flies and just about anything else.

Further, fishermen have vehemently argued all sorts of colors ranging from chartreuse to purple to green to red and ending up with black and white. We also argue about morning, afternoon and evening bites. Sunny versus cloudy days are also in the verbal arena.

Honestly, they'll hit just about anything. If I can say anything, it's that they'll hit aggressively for eight to ten casts and then suddenly turn off completely. It's usually a matter of changing colors or flies to turn them back on again. I've had the greatest luck with black egg-sucking leeches near the bottom. When they stop hitting, I switch to purple leeches. And when they stop again, I switch to something colorful. Constantly changing the colors and patterns is the key to successful silver fishing.

But, the truth be known, many times I've really scraped the bottom of my fly bag and come up with the most ungodly looking concoctions that have worked perfectly well. One time in Key West I bought a dozen of the ugliest tarpon flies I have ever seen. They were on sale for three dollars a dozen. How could I resist? I had them in my bag for at least five years and had never used them. They were ugly. The silvers, however, found them irresistible. Other times I used lures that were identical to rubber squids that also worked well.

I've also fished for them with dry flies, which some say is more exciting than using wet flies. There is something extraordinary about seeing a fifteen-pound fish slam a fly on the surface. My one disappointment with them, however, is their refusal to hit traditional trout flies like hoppers, Ausable Wulfs and other small stuff.

Sometimes they hold tight to cover, and precision casting is a necessity. Once they hit, I have to immediately drag them from the shores. Heavyweight line for this type of fishing is also a necessity. In general, I start with forty-pound line attached to the floating fly line. My tippet material is usually about twenty pounds. Anything less than fifteen-pound tippet material is asking for trouble. Sometimes the fish will be ten feet from shore or even just a few feet from me. Open-water fishing for them is great because they will usually run all over the place, including between your legs. And I can assure you that you'll lose significantly less equipment when you can get them to hit in open water.

My point is that there is no correct way to fish for them. When they're biting, they're biting. When they're not, they're not. I've caught more than eight hundred of them over the years and they still fascinate and mystify me. They are gifts from the fishing gods to fishermen who have done right in their lives.

My favorite way to fish for them is to find a shallow part of the river, about a foot deep or less. As they approach from downstream, their wakes really do appear to be a convoy of battle-ready navy destroyers. I then sight cast above them and let the line swing either near or directly into their convoy. Their charge on the fly is awe inspiring.

But getting them on the line is one thing. Getting them to the shore is another. A more explosive fish on the planet does not exist. I've had huge, twenty-pound silvers slam a fly just ten feet from me and easily jump six feet out of the water. They can scare the bejesus out of you. Often when they hit like this, they spit the hook right in your face.

They are violent and explosive. They can tear a hundred yards of line off your reel and take you deep into your backing. They often run circles around disbelieving fishermen. Many times they've also run right up on shore. They can also run toward snags and other cover and lose the hook on submerged branches and fallen trees. Or they'll twist and turn with such force that they'll break free. Their twisting and rolling action is affectionately known as the "silver shuffle" or the "silver twist."

Some people have likened them to ballet dancers. It's not in the least bit true. They're more like urban rap dancers on too much coffee. First-time silver salmon fishermen should be prepared for something astounding. Hang onto your hats!

In general, I use only hooks with the barbs removed. Fishing in this manner, however, requires special care. Tension must be kept on the line at all times or else the

[THIS PAGE-TOP] *The Tsiu River as seen from the air. The dark spots are salmon relaxing in quiet eddies.*
[THIS PAGE-BOTTOM] *Luke Conner casts for salmon in the shallow waters of the Tsiu River. The Wrangell Mountain Range and the Bering Glacier provide runoff water for the river.*

[THIS PAGE] *Seen from the air, the Tsiu and the Copper River flood plains provide almost unlimited areas for sport fishing.*
[OPPOSITE-TOP] *A large Dolly Varden taken on the Kenai River.*
[OPPOSITE-BOTTOM] *Also called reds because they "morph" into dramatic red colors, sockeye salmon school-up in quiet coves as they prepare for spawning and the end of their lives.*

hook will be spit in your face. Barbless hooks are significantly less damaging to the fish. They are also very easy to remove. I never use treble hooks. In my early years I did fish for them with a spinning rod but often cut two of the hooks off and crimped down the barb on the remaining hook. Barbless fishing is the only honorable way to fish for them. Absolute minimum harm should be done to them, and the fish should be gently and carefully returned to the water. Unless you're going to eat them!

Fighting a king salmon is like pulling up an old log from the bottom of a river. They just go down and tow you around. I've had very few large kings demonstrate the acrobatics often exhibited by silvers. On the other hand, fighting a silver, especially one fresh from the ocean, complete with a few straggling sea lice, is like trying to hold a hyperactive Irish setter on amphetamines that is trying to chase the neighborhood cats.

They are so violent that, in the past two years, I've broken four rods on them. I've had them make as many as seven major jumps. They are spectacular.

The best-tasting and the strongest silvers are taken directly from the sea or very near the mouths of the rivers. Once in the river, they stop eating and live off reserve fats. The farther upriver they go and the longer they've been in freshwater, the more lethargic they are. They attack things out of territoriality. I also believe that they take flies and other lures out of anger and meanness. They rule their world and have a "don't mess with me" attitude.

I've actually watched them slam into trout and other fish just to move them out of the rivers. Fully aware that trout eat their eggs, salmon want to rule their territory. They are the Mike Tysons of the fish world.

Once in freshwater, they are subject to an extremely rapid aging process. Within just a few hours they can become "blushed" with red colors. The males develop a very pronounced hooked jaw. Their one and only goal at the time they enter freshwater is to make it back to their place of hatching, have great sex and make as many baby salmon as possible. Then they roll over and die. They never see their kids, don't have to worry about college tuition and don't own Enron stock!

And so for the last week of August and the first week of September I hunt for these fish in the extraordinary waters off the Lost Coast of Alaska in the Prince William Sound area. The largest silvers come from the high-quality waters near the Copper River Basin and the Bering Ice Flows. It is a world-class fishery. They range between twelve and twenty-four pounds. It takes a significant amount of effort to get to these waters, so it's still a rather remote and pristine area. Only a few small fish camps exist in the region.

Back to the Kenai

Okay, I'm a glutton for punishment. On Saturday I returned to the Kenai one more time. I just couldn't get enough. But it's now September, the leaves are changing and almost all of the tourists have gone home. I met up with Tom Welsh from the Adirondacks and his cousin, Greg Kupchak. Greg's brother is the general manager for the Los Angeles Lakers, so we had to listen to basketball stories most of the day.

SEPTEMBER 7 Tom and Greg wanted to fish this evening, but I was too exhausted. They went without me. They returned to our cabin at Gwin's Lodge in Cooper Landing, after fishing the Russian River for a few hours. Tom proudly announced that he landed a big red Coho. "How disgusting," I thought. He seemed disappointed when I told him he had probably snagged the fish and reds don't count. Greg caught a great trout in a foot of water on a dry fly. It was their first time fishing in Alaska.

On Sunday morning we met fishing guide Fred Telleen for a day on the Kenai. We were after rainbows — big ones. We were on the water by eight-thirty in the morning. As expected, it first rained for a while, then it got hot, then sleet, then fog, then sunny, then more rain, then finally very cold and rainy; a typical day in Alaska.

I've never seen more reds in the Kenai. There were millions of bright red, humpbacked reds that would snag your line on every cast if not careful. A few of them were still living, but many were dead. Their rotting carcasses smelled to high heaven, but their lifeless bodies provided nutrients for the water and soil, food for the trout, bears, gulls, eagles and all sorts of other forms of life. I hooked several throughout the day and lost more line and gear than I care to remember.

We caught maybe twenty-five rainbows and Dolly Vardens each. Even though the fish weren't huge, the fishing was consistent and good. My largest rainbow was about twenty-two inches. Tom and Greg also caught a medium-sized silver each. They were thrilled and permanently hooked on silver fishing. It's called silver fever. Further, we tried several small streams off the Kenai, but the water was very low, and we found only a few magic spots. We looked forward to many more days of fishing.

SEPTEMBER 8 Fred Telleen met us at our cabin at 7 a.m. We were on the water within the hour. Fishing started slow. The biggest problem was that there were so many salmon eggs and carcasses in the water. Trout eat this stuff and they were full. Within two weeks the salmon would be gone and the trout fishing would be red hot. But we were here now and had no desire to wait. So we persisted in our efforts. Sometime in the morning, Tom landed a few good fish. Then a few hours later Greg and I caught a few huge Dollies off a seam of fast water. Both fish were sexually mature and had all their traditional bold markings.

Late in the afternoon we found ourselves fishing the confluence of Skilak Lake and the Kenai River. We fished the area for almost two hours before we caught our first fish. Greg finally found a small shoot of water no more than a foot deep that held fish willing to bite. Greg and I landed several big Dollies. It made our day.

Fishing the Kenai is an odd experience. It can only be likened to fishing with nymphs. It used to be that fishermen on this river fished with traditional flies. But then it dawned on some brilliant individual that the fish in these waters at this time of the year were eating nothing more than salmon eggs. So for a long time fishermen fished quite successfully with salmon eggs. Then some even brighter person thought the salmon eggs looked a lot like small plastic beads. So today everyone, and I mean everyone, fishes at this time of the year with small, plastic beads.

But I want to bring up something else that is important at this point: Fishing brings out all the neuroses, all the psychotic behaviors that most of us have been repressing and living with for years. It really does. I'm deadly serious when I say that if you're the least bit strange (that includes just about all of us), you really should try Prozac or Zoloft or Wellbutrin or some other antidepressants before you go fishing. I'm not kidding. I'll tell you why.

If you fish with friends, or anyone else for that matter, and they're catching fish left and right, and you're not, then crazy things will start to happen in your head. The first thing is that you'll get very quiet. Everyone else is talking and having a great time but you get quiet. You hate that you're not catching fish. It means that you're not as good as everyone else, that there is something wrong with you. It doesn't mean that you're just down on your luck, but that you are not as able as the next guy is; that they are better than you are.

[OPPOSITE] *Once the spawn is complete, hundreds of thousands of salmon die. Their carcasses either line the shoreline or decompose on the bottom of the river. The nutrients from their bodies allow life in many forms to go on.*

[PHOTO SERIES] *We all know that moose are dangerously ferocious; so when a moose waded into the river, the fishermen held still for a few seconds. But in the last picture, you'll see that everybody went on with their business, including the moose.*

Then you think about how much you hate the people you're fishing with. You can't stand them. You never want to see them again. If they are your employees, you think about firing them or at least cutting their salary. If they are your in-laws, you think about getting a divorce.

You think of giving up the sport. You think of going home early. You make up excuses. You think of breaking your equipment. You think something is wrong with you. You hate everyone. God and the angels have abandoned you. You did something wrong in another life and the fish gods are getting back at you. And if your fishing buddies keep having a great time and you continue on with your fishless ways, you think of things that can easily send you to prison. You get quieter. You get weird. You are now dangerous.

But then you catch a fish and then another and then another. Then you catch a few really big ones! A smile returns to your face. You laugh and talk again. You calm down. Things are okay again. But then the other people stop catching fish and they begin the hellacious descent into mental chaos. It's now their turn to be miserable.

I call this syndrome Fishing Bipolar Disease (FBD). Its manifestations are violent mood swings, manic depression and a host of other symptoms. If you suffer from FBD, you have three choices: (1) You can go in for long-term therapy, (2) you can try antidepressants, or (3) you can give up fishing altogether.

Personally, I haven't decided which therapy I should partake in, but I know I need one of them.

There is another thing to be worried about. Bears. You probably noticed that I'm a bit concerned about big bruins. The word *paranoid* comes to mind. The word actually means "unnecessary fear." But I don't think my concerns are unnecessary. Bears really scare me, and they kill people. So instead of paranoid may I suggest *bearanoid?* The word has two and maybe three clever meanings. The first suggests a real fear of bears. The second refers to being annoyed by bears. And maybe a third use for the term is that the bears are actually annoyed by us. Whatever the case, it's best to use good judgment around these creatures. I know I do.

The more I fish in the wilds, the less fear I have of bears. I still have profound respect for them, but in reality, they want nothing to do with us. Usually just a shout sends them running. But I'm still waiting for a false charge from a thousand-pound grizzly that stops just ten feet from me. When it's over, just start CPR on me and call an ambulance. I can assure you that my heart will have given way. My will is in the top left-hand drawer of my desk.

SEPTEMBER 9 I was up most of the night. I missed my family, and I was still struggling from my earlier bout with FBD. Sometimes valleys run too deep. It also depends on how well you're getting along with the people you're fishing with. In truth, sometimes I think Tom and Greg are "wackos," and I wondered what I was doing in Alaska with them. Fred met us at 6 a.m. We were going to fish the section of the Kenai River just below Skilak Lake. The morning was cold at forty degrees but beautiful with sunny skies. We traveled across the lake toward the fish. I panned the horizon. No one else was around. I was happy to be there.

The first fish within five minutes of fishing was a big Dolly. I caught it on an imitation salmon egg. It was a great battle. We fished along a line of sandbars that were incredibly productive. I fished there earlier in the year and caught many great rainbows. The loons were calling. The eagles sat on the bank and ate leftovers from the gorging of bears that haunt the area at night, and a flock of

trumpeter swans rode majestically on the water's edge near towering Sitka spruce trees. It was a magical place. Life was good.

We caught more huge Dollies. Dolly Vardens got their name from a character from a Charles Dickens novel. Our guide, Fred Telleen, informed us that a few years earlier he had guided the granddaughter of the individual who actually named Dollies "Dollies." Apparently, in the 1930s a man at the McCloud Fish Hatchery in California found a strange-looking fish in a large batch of rainbows that had just been netted. It had purple highlights and polka dots. It reminded him of the Dickens character Dolly Varden. The name stuck. If anyone has a different version of the story, I would love to hear it!

Throughout the day I missed two huge rainbows. Everything has to be right to successfully land these guys. Both fish were above twenty-six inches. I was disappointed, but I just continued fishing. I have a tendency not to dwell on milk already spilled. I know what not to do next time.

Tom caught many fish and a huge rainbow. He and his cousin, Greg, enjoyed fishing for silvers. We found two holes full of these guys and fished for them for more than an hour. Tom caught several and I took a few, including a surprise chromed male fresh from the ocean. To the disappointment of my cohorts, I released him to complete the apex of his life. For him to come so far and to deny him the final few days of his life would have been a sin. I had enough to eat and enough salmon in my freezer. No need to kill more. My one surprise, however, was how beautiful the silvers become once they mature to a dark, rich red worthy of admiration by all.

Greg, the third member of our group, was new to fly-fishing. A huge man, he sometimes struggled with his casting. He did improve dramatically throughout the trip. Because he could not initially cast with completely accurate precision, he often landed in a school of spent pink salmon, also affectionately called "humpies." He caught more of these creatures than Tom and I together. But as the day went on, we all seemed to tangle with these guys.

So to make matters a little lighter, we developed a contest that many may find useful and interesting. Although we tried our best not to catch them, fair-hooked humpies were worth five points,

[THIS PAGE-LEFT] *Nets are often essential as it's necessary to retrieve and release fish as quickly as possible.*
[THIS PAGE-CENTER] *Guide Fred Telleen struggles to handle a monster rainbow trout. Such fish are easily termed "the fish of a lifetime!"*
[THIS PAGE-RIGHT] *Heather Wollschleger shows off a good-sized silver salmon.*
[OPPOSITE] *Combat fishing on the Kenai.*

foul-hooked humpies were worth two. Dead ones were worth a half-point each. The winner would receive free cocktails for the rest of the evening. That night we had to take the car keys from Greg. We put him to bed around 10 p.m. We hoped he would have no hangover.

Humpies are the bane of Alaskan fishermen. They get no respect. Greg was kind enough, however, to pay homage to them. He was for the underdog, he repeatedly said. And I can assure you that humpies are the underdogs.

Perhaps the most bizarre and strangest-looking fish to come inland, I can see absolutely no logical reason why they morph into the fish they become. Ecologically, it's just not necessary. Their humps are huge and their jaws are stranger than strange. But there is a certain sense of humor to them. Their comical appearance should be looked upon with interest and not disdain. They should be highly regarded as unique and with character rather than with the scorn that they presently receive. However we perceive them, I'm glad to say that in two hours of fishing I only received ninety-six points in our recent first-annual "Humpy Power" contest.

SEPTEMBER 11   The day started with remembrance of the past year's events. A year ago I was in a hotel room. I was speaking with someone from the Reddington Fly Rod Company. He told me to hang up and turn on the TV. To the horror of all Americans, we were under attack. Being from New York and having many of my clients and friends working in the financial sector at the World Trade Center, I could only imagine the terror of the day.

So on this morning in Alaska, I could only sit and remember with sadness, the events of the past year. After breakfast we watched TV for a while. The president was at a memorial service in Pennsylvania. We watched for a while and I must admit that I had to leave. It was far too emotional for me to watch. I worry when my car doesn't start or I have to shovel snow from my front porch. In truth, I really have no problems. My own troubles are completely insignifi-

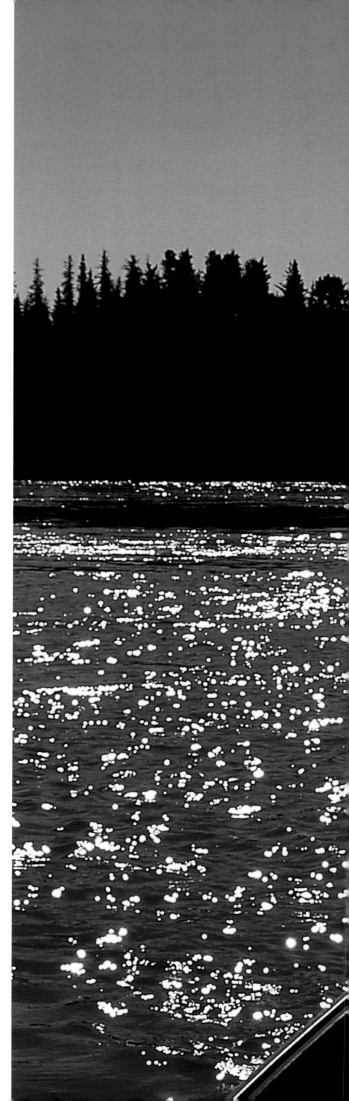

cant compared to the horrors and travails experienced by those affected and connected with the attacks. I count my blessings. And I offer my hopes and condolences to those closely touched by the tragedy.

And so with these thoughts in mind, I felt a pang of guilt as I went fishing. Nonetheless, it's critical that life goes on.

So without a guide, Tom, Greg and I wandered down to a gravel bar on the Kenai. We rigged our lines with plastic eggs and cast in. Greg got the first fish. And the second and the third and on and on. He had at least ten and I had yet to catch anything. Tom got a bunch as well. I was prepared for the return of FBD but took things under control. I changed the hook, the egg, the length of my tippet, the color and length of my strike indicator, position on the river, everything. In life, as in fishing, it's necessary to take control and make changes once in a while. I even stood right next to Greg in hopes of "weaseling" a few fish out of his spot. Still, there was nothing. Despite my best efforts, no fish came my way.

In the early afternoon it started to rain, and we were forced to return to our cabin. After considerable contemplation of our choices, which included either doing laundry or going fishing in the rain, we put on our foul-weather gear and returned to the river.

So for three more hours we again fished the banks of the mighty Kenai River. Greg caught a beautiful silver and many large rainbows. Tom caught several big rainbows above twenty inches and a grayling. I caught nothing. As the old expression goes, "Sometimes you're the fire hydrant, and sometimes you're the dog," or something like that. Better days would come.

SEPTEMBER 12   I woke up exhausted. I had been traveling too much. I missed my family and my home. My hands were sore and I was cold. Even though I had paid for another trip on the Kenai with guide Fred Telleen, I decided to stay in my cabin. As I had no vehicle, I stayed near the camp complex. After two hours of moping around, I was bored. I called my wife. She was out. I took several naps throughout the day. I had a bowl of Gwin's famous seafood chowder for lunch and then went for a hike. I returned to the cabin and spent the rest of the day writing. It's good to be productive.

SEPTEMBER 13   I'm in Alaska, so I'm going fishing. I will not be denied. It costs too much to get here and I will probably not return for a while. It's raining outside. And it's still dark. Inside, the snoring continues. It's a nightmare. Fred will be here at 7 a.m. It's now time to put on waders and get ready.

I walked out of the door at 7:02 a.m. Fred was walking toward the cabin, fully anticipating that he would have to wake me up, but I was ready to boogie!

I fished with three individuals that I had never met before. We met and all were congenial, including Ian, a whiz-kid fisherman. Shortly, we were on the river. Fishing started fast today. I took my first rainbow minutes after we launched. Within a mile, we found a bank and stayed there for the rest of the day. The fishing did not stop. It was one right after the other. I caught numerous fish in the twenty-two- to twenty-four-inch range. And I lost a few others that were larger than that. Most of the trout that were caught were so fat that they looked like footballs.

Ian caught not only rainbows but many silvers throughout the day, as well. In his town of Girdwood, Alaska, he's a local legend. People followed him to see where he was fishing. He's caught over a thousand silvers since the beginning of his fishing career. He's only fifteen.

But while I was out there on the Kenai, I realized that there were other diseases that afflict fishermen, along with FBD. Another is called BSFD. It's a terrible disease. It affects ninety-five percent of all fishermen.

The real name for it is Back Seat Fisherman's Disease (BSFD). Everyone has it and we have all been subjected to it at some time or another as fishermen! Here are the manifestations: The next time you get a fish on the line, listen for just a moment to what others around you are saying. For example, you'll hear:

"Keep the rod tip up."

"Take up the slack."

"The drag is too tight."

"Loosen the drag."

"Tighten the drag."

"Reel in."

"Don't pull so hard."

"Walk backwards."

"Pull harder."

None of these suggestions mean anything. They're just the ravings and incantations of people who are jealous because someone other than themselves has a fish on the line. It's best to just ignore them and go about your own business of bringing in the fish.

Some people really get carried away with this affliction. Their soul purpose is to inflict guilt on you. Sometimes they raise their voices not only during the fish fight but also after the fish has been lost. The worst I ever heard was from a guide on the Kenai this past summer. I mean he really screamed and hollered at his clients when they did something "wrong." After listening to him I was surprised he was still in business. Frankly, I would never hire him to guide me. He really needed antidepressants and long-term therapy.

There is another malady that I should probably bring up. It's called the LFS, or the Lost Fish Syndrome. It's stuff people say to themselves and to others after they've lost a fish. It sounds like this:

"I set the hook too soon."

"I pulled the hook right out of its mouth."

"The drag was set too tight."

"The drag was set too loose."

"The hook was too dull."

[OPPOSITE-BOTTOM] *This salmon had been hooked several times. The various lures stuck in his mouth were removed before he was released.*
[THIS PAGE] *Fred Telleen displays a healthy salmon taken off the Kenai River in Alaska.*

"My line broke because I set the hook too hard."

"I let him go into the weeds."

"I should'a done this."

"I should'a done that."

Fishermen tear themselves apart when they lose a fish. The mental battle goes on and on. It can last for months and even years. We can beat ourselves up twenty-four hours a day on this kind of stuff. It doesn't stop. This obsessive behavior also calls for long-term therapy.

Throughout the day it rained. The temperature hovered around fifty and the wind blew hard. I caught a chill in the morning and was not able to warm up as the day progressed. I had four peanut butter cups and a bottle of Power Aid for lunch. By 4 p.m. I was wet and tired. I had dinner by myself at Gwin's and then wandered up to the cabin for some sleep.

SEPTEMBER 14   We were supposed to go to the Anchor River at five this morning. The trip had to be postponed because the people I'm traveling with could not find the energy to get up. They partied until late in the night. The miserable morning after is the price they pay. I am disappointed and irritated. In the afternoon we drove down to Homer, Alaska. There we had a delicious dinner of scallops at a local restaurant and then a cocktail or two at my all-time favorite tavern, the Lighthouse Inn.

As mentioned, Greg and Tom are big fellows, each is six feet, six inches and each weighs over 260. There is not an ounce of fat on either of them. Greg also wears a massive championship gold and diamond ring given to him by his brother, who manages the Los Angeles Lakers. Everyone wants to meet him and wear, just for a few minutes, "THE RING." Tom wears two long earrings and a ponytail. Women flock to these two guys. I usually wind up sitting alone as the "boys" enjoy the flirtatious company of the locals. I'm usually awestruck at how lucky they get. But I have a great wife and daughter at home and behave myself.

One fortunate circumstance of being very good friends with both of them is that I feel completely safe, even in the occasional seedy bar we might find our way to. Little guys like myself are often on the receiving end of some drunkard's wrath. I see these two guys as my guardian angels.

SEPTEMBER 15   We started out the day with a drive up to Deep Creek, about twenty minutes north of Homer. I used my five-weight rod with a plastic bead as bait. Deep Creek is a small stream, maybe twenty feet across at its widest. I saw several carcasses on the shores and the river is well known by locals for steelhead and silver. After two hours, nothing came my way.

Greg caught two smaller Jack (male) silvers on an egg pattern. Unfortunately, he slipped twice and landed in the water, up to his shoulders both times. To his and our dismay, during the fiasco, he succeeded in losing his wallet. Needless to say, he was deeply troubled by this, and we literally spent the rest of the day searching the waters. Thinking that he could have left his wallet elsewhere, we also returned to our cabin and the restaurant where we had breakfast, looking for his billfold. It was to no avail; he finally gave up the ghost and realized that it was lost forever. To make matters worse, his only picture ID was in the wallet. Fully aware that he could not board the airplane for his flight home on the following day without a picture ID, he sought advice from the local police. He was also concerned because the registration for his handgun that he had with him was in his wallet, thus complicating matters.

So if you're ever fishing Deep Creek, just off the Sterling Highway, and you find a wallet containing $1,500 in cash, IDs and other papers, please feel free to contact the name of the individual on the driver's license. There is a fifty-dollar reward for the return of the cash and the contents of the wallet!

That night, we wound up on Homer Spit. Greg and I took a flight-seeing trip over the glaciers, fjords and islands in a mint-condition 1929 Travel Air 6000B bush aircraft on Edo floats powered by a 420-horsepower Curtis Wright engine. I know this because Greg gave me an hour lecture on the plane even before we signed up for the trip. Greg knew more about antique aircraft than any person I ever met. He and the seventy-three-year-old pilot seemed to be in heaven as they discussed the subtle nuances of the aircraft. Frankly, however, as we flew low over huge glaciers and extremely close to mountain walls I wished Greg would have shut up and allowed the pilot to concentrate on flying the plane rather than gabbing.

After the flight, we met Tom at the pond on the spit where he and a hundred others were snagging silvers. Yearly, the town of Homer places around a hundred thousand salmon fry in a tidal pool off the spit. To the amusement and pleasure of the tourists and locals, a few years later the adult silvers return. For the first week of their return, everyone is allowed to fish for them. At the end of the week, snagging with treble hooks is allowed. It's a rather disgusting spectacle. But considering that the fish will be dead in a few days, I suppose its best to have them on someone's dinner table rather than let them rot on the beach. Nonetheless, it still bothers me. There is no art to it. I will comment no further on the spectacle lest I infuriate the good people of Homer, Alaska.

The following morning we were up at five. Tom insisted on snagging another day's limit of silvers at the pond. So at sunrise we had breakfast and then returned to the spit for another few hours of butchering. By noon we had each caught our limit of six. We had lunch and then made our way back to our hotel room to pack. Unfortunately, we were to have checked out by eleven and we were already two hours late. I had to leave a big tip for the housemaid, and we were lucky to have avoided paying for another night's stay.

Because we were cheap and this was a budget trip, we had rented a mid-size car. We actually needed a truck and trailer to haul all the gear Tom and Greg brought with them. Once we were finally packed, there was hardly room for the two giants I was traveling with. I had to literally slam the doors shut on both of the guys, as they were so crammed into the vehicle. Greg had to sit with more than a hundred pounds of salmon on his lap for the two-hour drive to the fish-processing house.

Meat hunters are mentally bereft. I don't understand their logic. Frankly, there is none when it comes to meat hunting. As I have listened to numerous hunters and fishermen, they argue that the reason they go fishing is to put fresh meat on the table. But truthfully, the finances and realities don't add up. Stop and think about this: To go fishing in Alaska costs a fortune. By the time you buy an

RED SALMON LODGE
595-2000 VACANCY
NO VACANCY

TROUTFITTERS
ALPINE MOTEL
TROPHY TACKLE

DRIFTERS LODGE
ROOMS CABINS
595-5555
VACANCY
GUIDED FISHING

ALASKA
TROUT FITTERS
DRIFT BOAT RENTALS RAFT RENTALS
GUIDED FISHING

[OPPOSITE] *Fly fisherman Greg Kupchak battles a silver salmon on the quiet waters of the Kenai River. Guide Fred Telleen patiently waits for the right moment to release the fish.*

airplane ticket, and pay for car rental, hotels, guides, fishing gear, meals, tips, souvenirs, etc., you have spent a fortune. It's far cheaper to go to the grocery store and buy fresh salmon in the fish department.

Other people argue that they don't like frozen food. So they go out, catch a hundred pounds of salmon, freeze it and then wait four months before they finish all of it. It's far better to go to the store to buy fresh food.

Nonetheless, once Greg and Tom got the bill of five hundred dollars for cleaning, smoking, shrink-wrapping, gel packs (for freezing), a box and overnight shipping for their sixty pounds of fish, they just about fell over. If you add up all the bills, their smoked fish came to about four hundred dollars a pound!

We finally made our way to the airport in Anchorage. Tom and I were on the same flight that was leaving at 1:20 a.m. We were up all night. It was a full flight, and it was impossible to sleep. I sat next to a middle-aged woman who complained of an unusual smell to the attendant. I had not done my laundry in a week and my clothes stunk of fish.

The entire day was straight from hell. My bones and joints ached from sitting on a plane. We finally arrived back in Lake George at 6 p.m. Tom drove home. I did my laundry, responded to fifty-three e-mails, put together a slide show, repacked my bags, slept for two hours and then returned to the airport in Albany at 5 a.m. with Michele and Lindsey. We then sat on three more planes throughout the day and eventually landed in Cody, Wyoming.

Although busy in the summer, the Kenai offers numerous quiet feeder streams and has-stunning scenery year-round.

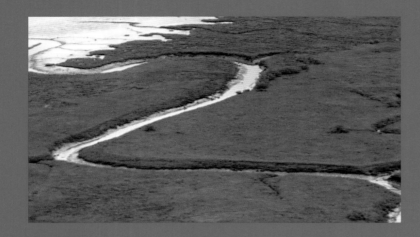

THE KATALLA

The companionship
and camaraderie
that camps afford
is the essence
of these
adventures.

Cordova, Alaska, is the jumping-off point for

this adventure. Several small B&Bs exist in the town. My favorite is the Orca Adventure Lodge, owned by Steve Ranney. Steve and his mother, Laura, are legends in Alaska as bush pilots. Their lodge offers very comfortable rooms, exceptional meals, a charter service and guides, as well as remote camps for some of the most extraordinary adventures imaginable. Located on the scenic coast of Alaska, killer whales, seals, eagles and sea otters can easily be seen from the front porch of the Cordova Lodge.

[THIS PAGE] *The Lost Coast of Alaska is known for its impressive runs of trophy-size silver salmon. The remoteness of this region favors the fisherman who is willing to travel extended distances for the experience of a lifetime.*

[OPPOSITE-LEFT] *There is no doubt about the presence of huge bears around just about every river in Alaska. The proximity of such bears requires fishermen and visitors to use extreme caution.*
[OPPOSITE-CENTER] *Brian Correll happily shows off an eighteen-pound silver salmon taken on a five-weight fly rod on the Katalla River.*
[OPPOSITE-RIGHT] *Standing proudly with a silver salmon taken on a dry fly on the Katalla River.*

Several others and I flew into their remote camp to fish for mighty silver salmon on the isolated Katalla River. The flight in was spectacular. The Copper River delta, as seen from the air, is an abstract painting far superior to any artwork ever created by mere humans. Landing on the Katalla River airstrip (it really doubles as a goat path) always takes my breath away. Look out for the bears! Beach landings are at least tolerable. I'm always happy, however, when I'm back on the ground.

Once at the camp, I met my old friend and fishing guide, Luke Conner. Luke is the best caster I have ever seen. He is the ultimate fishing guide and knows more about the wilderness than people three times his age. We also met guide Dave Salmon. Dave has a Ph.D. in oceanography and works as a commercial fisherman during the rest of the year. His intimate knowledge of the lives of salmon and the oceans in which they live was insightful. Dave and I became good friends during my visit. The experience of these two guides guaranteed adventure.

For seven straight days we fished for silvers morning to night. We were not disappointed. It was not uncommon to catch a fish on every other cast. Many times I would go for ten straight casts and land a fish each time. Further, it was very common for the group to have doubles, triples and even quadruples at the same time. It was exhausting work!

The camp was rustic in nature. As these facilities are usually open for no more than eight weeks a year, it does not pay to have ultra-modern accommodations. Nonetheless, we were dry, warm and comfortable for the week we were there. The food was delicious and plentiful, the scenery was out of this world, and the fishing was beyond belief.

For anyone who attends these camps, one thought should be foremost in their minds: You should not wander off looking for new adventures. This is absolute wilderness with no street signs, fences or neighbors. Cell phones don't work there, and there are no friendly policemen to ask for help when needed. On many occasions, bears, really big ones, are there for the viewing. They just wander right

on in, so a constant look over your shoulder is strongly advised. When they do show up (and they do), it's necessary to not freak out. Just make noise and they'll leave you alone. They only want the salmon, not you. Guides all pack heavy firearms and frequently have to have them unholstered for the many bears that happen to wander in. Wolves are also plentiful and the landscape can swallow you up so fast you won't believe it. So be careful and don't do anything stupid.

One example of how suddenly bears can appear happened on the Tsiu River that we fished for a day during this trip. A hundred yards down from us, we saw what at first appeared to be a large horse at full gallop. It turned out to be a huge brown bear. Its speed was shocking. It charged right into a group of ten fishermen, who no doubt were casually enjoying their afternoon. Upon seeing the charging bear, the men scattered like bowling pins bouncing off a bowling ball. The bear charged right in, grabbed a salmon and then retreated. It was the funniest thing to watch, but please believe me when I say I was very happy the bear was in another camp and not ours.

The true nature of these experiences is not the fish or the food or the scenery. Rather, the companionship and the camaraderie that such camps afford is the essence of these adventures. My fishing buddies have become like family members. To fish side by side with friends and to share both dangers and adventures for days is cathartic.

Realistically, however, the chemistry has to be right. One or two people with different personalities can alter everything. That's why I also tell people not to have political discussions in camp. Differences of opinion can often ruin an experience.

On the next to last day of this trip, it rained. All of us were tired, our bones ached and our hands were sore and full of cuts and bruises. We had caught enough fish and we needed a day off anyway. So we built a fire and spent the next eight hours talking of our lives and our hopes for the future. One individual, a Japanese American, told of his life being interned in a camp during

[BOTTOM] *Steve Ranney and his mother, both experienced bush pilots, stand in front of one of their planes in Cordova, Alaska. They are owners of the Orca Adventure Lodge, which offers high-quality fishing trips and accommodations in the Lost Coast region of Alaska.*

the Second World War. Another gentleman told us of his grand-kids and his battle with cancer. Another man told of the tragic loss of his daughter to breast cancer. And another old friend, a retired school principal, talked of the loss of a great teacher and how it affected the kids in his school. There was not a dry eye in the room.

But these were the stories of our lives. We all agreed that none of us were getting any younger and we all needed the occasional strength of others to find meaning in our lives. Eventually, we said that the strength we often gather from others helps us to go on.

I left the camp late that afternoon feeling rejuvenated from the adventure and also honored and privileged to have friends who were willing to share their lives with others. It was profound and humbling. I've always felt more human and more comfortable with myself when such things occur. Maturation happens not because we are getting older, but rather as a function of interacting with others. Things like that happen in fishing camps. It's a good thing.

[TOP] *One of many wilderness cabins offered by Orca Adventure Lodge in the interior of Alaska.*
[MIDDLE] *Colorful salmon flies are the staple of fly fishermen seeking big salmon.*
[BOTTOM] *Trophy-size salmon are the reward for fishiing the Lost Coast.*

Flying over the Lost Coast one has the opportunity to see hundreds of rivers that snake their way toward the ocean. Rivers such as this are usually full of salmon returning to their home waters.

[OPPOSITE-TOP AND BOTTOM LEFT] *Silvers are known as bruising fighters and often jump five or six times to the astonishment and delight of fishermen.*
[OPPOSITE-BOTTOM RIGHT] *On the last day of a recent trip, several fishermen decided to return home with their limit of silvers. Here, guide Luke Conner, the fastest filleter in the West, cleans fish and readies them for the smokehouse!*

YELLOWSTONE TO JACKSON

My first
cast
across the
calm water
fell
perfectly.

It's now early in the morning here at Old Faithful

Inn. People are again asleep and I'm writing this to the sound of a crackling fire that roars in the fireplace three stories below me. I've noticed with concern, the aging of the inn. The floors are sagging a bit more and its old hallowed halls are showing signs of further wear. I hope that every effort is taken to maintain the building, as it is one of America's great historic rustic structures.

Arguably the most technically challenging river in the West, the Fire Hole in Yellowstone National Park is complete with raging rapids and deep holes. Here an experienced fly fisherman crouches low as he casts a fly for trout.

[159]

We ate breakfast yesterday morning in the dining hall. It was a large buffet. I tried to limit my intake of eggs. Afterwards, we rode up to a meadow and watched a herd of bison for quite some time. It was rutting season and the bulls were in rare form. They are massive and at the height of their aggressiveness, and we watched in awe as battles raged between competing males. A crowd of people gathered to watch the spectacle, and several times the bison battled between vehicles, forcing us puny humans to seek the insecure safety of our cars.

I found a quiet spot along the Fire Hole River. Certainly one of the most famous rivers in the West, the Fire Hole is beautiful, awe inspiring, dangerous and technically challenging. There is also significant thermal activity on the river. Geysers and mud holes spew endless streams of hot, sulfur-laden water into the river. The banks are incredibly dangerous. Ground along the river is thin, and fishermen break through the surface and receive life-threatening, third-degree burns every year.

One must know the local ecology well to catch fish here. Fished heavily throughout the three warm seasons, trout in the Fire Hole have seen everything humans can throw at them. They are not dumb. And because the eagles and osprey hunt the shallow river, the fish are leery of sitting in open waters. Walking along the banks, I've often thrown live grasshoppers into the water to see what the fish are eating. I've also fished it with caddis flies, nymphs, dry flies of all sorts and just about everything else. Despite this, in the years I've fished the Fire Hole, I've only caught two fish — a rather dismal record, if I must say so.

Another small stream that flows through the park is the Nez Perce. The author is seen here casting to a few holes while a herd of bison graze nearby.

One more thing to worry about is that quicksand is also found in the area. When wandering in unknown places, I walk in the footsteps of the buffalo or elk. If the ground can support the weight of one of those eight-hundred-pound behemoths, then it should be able to support a few overweight fishermen. But despite these things, the river is inviting and immediately accessible. As we drive along with the river at our side, I'm compelled to stop and "throw a few." The elk and bison are always there and the scenery will take your breath away. The Fire Hole is a good river to keep one humble.

At 1 p.m. I met with George from the Old Faithful Inn. We drove just a few miles north to the Nez Perce River, a small, meandering stream. We walked upriver just a hundred yards or so and threw in our lines. The water was less than a foot deep and only a few inches in many places. I watched the water carefully and finally saw a few small fish rising. We fished for eight- to ten-inch brookies and browns. I started with hoppers and finally ended up throwing tiny number-twenty nymphs. Although the fish were rising and feeding on something, neither George nor I was successful in connecting with them.

We returned to the inn a few hours later where I met up with my wife and daughter, and we drove back to the Fire Hole for an evening's worth of fishing. Still no fish. I asked several other fly throwers about their efforts and each reported minimal luck. I remain humble and content in the thought that fly-fishing is not always about catching fish.

OCTOBER 24 It's 4 a.m. and we're in Jackson, Wyoming. As usual, I'm up and wide awake. Rather than turn on the TV and disturb my wife and daughter, I work on my laptop. The drive down from Yellowstone was stunning. The trees were in full bloom and animals were visible everywhere. The local newspaper reported that a grizzly had attacked an experienced guide in the Teton Mountains not far from where we are staying. There is no changing the wildness of this place. Later today we'll fish the Green River in an isolated, rural part of the state. The water is reported to be low and the big browns are in. We'll see.

It's now evening. It was a strange day. We finally left our hotel room at around 8 a.m. We drove a good ninety minutes south of Jackson to an almost-impossible-to-find dirt turnoff and then almost an hour along a road that should have been condemned. But eventually we found the right spot, a remote section of the Green River.

The short walk from the road to the river was plagued with badger holes, rattlesnakes, cow dung, and antelope poop. The river looked great, though — absolutely clear. And no wind! As I walked, I noticed thousands of hoppers. They had light yellow bellies. They, I surmised, would be my ticket to success. So for the next hour I threw light yellow-bellied hoppers on seams, behind rocks, under branches, on calm water, on fast water . . . nothing. Figuring it must be the location, we loaded up and drove upstream about a mile. This time I tried any number of dry flies and, adding a small nymph onto the fly. Still nothing. So we packed up again and drove another mile upstream. After nearly five hours of fishing, we still had nothing.

I found myself descending into the abyss of fishing hell. Fishing like this is not therapeutic. Introspective maybe, but far from therapeutic. Should I try farther upstream, or should I stay where I was? Should I try different bait? Was I violating some law of fishing I wasn't even aware of? Fishless fishing is a self-tormenting hell, and I was digging deep. Why didn't I have more patience? Why

couldn't I stay still? Maybe what Mrs. Case, my third grade teacher who told me I was a lousy speller and I would never amount to anything, said was true. Maybe it's because I had flunked high school Algebra One four times. Maybe (I was scraping the bottom of self-pity now) it was because my parents fought in front of me all the time.

Interrupting my torment, my wife called me to come have lunch. She will never realize how her one simple statement saved me. Gratefully, I ate a sandwich, played with my daughter and then packed up for the day.

We drove to the end of the road. I turned the car around, ready to leave. "Ralph, this looks like a great spot. Take a few more casts," Michele said to me. At that moment she was an angel and her words of encouragement manna from heaven. She did not have to twist my arm.

I reassembled my rod and wandered into the stream. The water was calm. Beds of seaweed flowed gracefully with the slow current. My first cast across the calm water fell perfectly. I relaxed and enjoyed the feel of the fly rod in my hand again. With a few more casts I played the line upstream with a graceful mend.

On my fifth cast I could see the flash just as the hopper hit the water. The fish slammed the fly violently. It jumped five times, right in the sun, so I could not determine what it was. I prayed it was not a whitefish. But whitefish don't slam big flies on the sur- face. My daughter giggled when I brought the fish near the shore and I let her reel the last few feet. It was an eighteen-inch light- colored brown trout.

We made photos of the fish and released it to the safety of the water. The fish gods had smiled on me. I forgot all the mental garbage and relaxed again. Catching fish brings me down to earth.

The thought occurred to me that for the past month I had been fishing in Alaska. And Alaska will forever spoil people. Twenty- inch fish on every other cast is almost the norm up there — you come to expect it. It's almost inevitable that when you fish else- where, you will experience disappointment.

It's necessary to keep that in mind when you don't land a hundred fish a day. It's not personal, it's just that rivers in the lower forty- eight have been subject to fishermen throwing all kinds of flies in the river for generations and the fish are used to it!

Inside Yellowstone National Park flows the Fire Hole River. Complete with geysers, quick- sand and hot water, the river is a stunning sight as it flows gracefully through the park. In ten years of fishing the river I've caught only two small trout.

October 7

THE HOH RIVER

Like all fishermen, I wouldn't say no to anything that tugged on my line.

I had just driven about nine hours from Maine

to get back to my home in New York. I was happy to play with my daughter, who insisted on singing nearly fifty verses of "I See the Moon." By 10 p.m. my wife had to put me to bed. Tomorrow we would be on our way for three weeks of steelhead fishing in Washington State and on Vancouver Island, British Columbia.

I awoke at 2 a.m. I call it the dead zone — I can't call anyone or go anywhere. But I use the time productively to write, answer e-mails and faxes, practice blues and jazz on my bass guitar and occasionally read.

[ABOVE] *Guide Pat Graham throws a long cast on the Hoh River in the Olympia Rain Forest. If fishing for winter-run steelhead, sinking tip line and weighted flies are used to get to the bottom of the river where the fish congregate.*

[165]

Michele got up with me and finished the laundry and packing. Usually, within a few hours I go back to sleep but not today. At 6 a.m. we loaded the car with our luggage, toys and clothes for our daughter, camera gear and, finally, fishing equipment. By nine we were on a plane headed first for the West Coast.

Usually, all my joints ache after a long flight. Today I was sick of airplanes and airport terminals. I was sick of the six peanuts or the twelve mini-pretzels they give you for lunch. And the last six flights I have been on have shown the same movie; to this day, I can't stand Hugh Grant, his exaggerated accent or his blow-dried hairdo.

Finally, we arrived in Seattle. We were going to be joined by my sister-in-law, Tina Keller, who lives in Chicago. Tina often acts as our daughter's nanny and gives us some time off for ourselves to go fishing. But traveling with Tina also comes at a price: She is notorious for bringing several large suitcases with her, no matter how long the trip is. She has to have two hair dryers, curling irons and at least three changes of clothes per day. Her makeup bag alone could easily fill a large suitcase. She argues that I bring along several different fishing poles, so she should be able to bring along her gear as well. Although I have long stopped fighting with her, I find that I have to rent a very large full-size car or van when she comes along. I also have to wait inordinate amounts of time while she does her hair and irons her clothes. But she is family and I occasionally enjoy her company. And she does take good care of Lindsey.

We picked up the rental car and waited around for Tina's plane to arrive. We were finally loaded and ready to go by nine that night, but within just a few minutes of driving, we all agreed to find a local hotel, get a good night's sleep and head out for the river in the morning. This required me bringing all of Tina's luggage to her room, of course. I am perfectly happy with just my toothbrush, but she has to have her entire wardrobe. She is the only person I know in the world who has to wash her hair twice a day.

In the morning we made our way toward the Olympic Rain Forest; we stopped in Port Angeles for a terrific seafood lunch. We traveled past beautiful Crescent Lake and into the rain forest with its towering, moss-covered old-growth trees. It was good to be there — it felt safe.

Finally we arrived at the Huckleberry Lodge in the town of Forks, Washington. The setting was clean, well maintained, and perfectly groomed. We had a modern cabin to ourselves amidst the towering trees and green grass. After taking more than an hour to unload the vehicle, I soaked for a long time in the hot tub overlooking the meandering Calawah River.

As I looked at the terrain, I was happy to know that there were no grizzly bears anywhere around. The environs were perfect for them, and in the past this had been part of their home range, but not any longer. I immediately felt more comfortable. Then I read the large warning in our cabin about cougars. Cougars were all over the place, and they had been known to attack people. The sign read "BEWARE." There is no rest for the wicked!

OCTOBER 10 I awoke at five, dressed, and met guide Pat Graham for breakfast at six. Kitty Sperry, co-owner of the Huckleberry Lodge, served us a great breakfast of waffles with all the trimmings. Just as I was all set to go, she brought out a second plate of eggs, bacon, potatoes and other goodies. My guide inhaled this segment of his breakfast as well and then several cups of coffee. On the way to the river, he stopped and purchased a huge bottle of Mountain Dew and consumed it during the drive. If I had drunk that much caffeine, I would have been up for the rest of the week!

It was a foggy morning. Elk were everywhere and mist hung on the huge trees. The final drive up to the river was nothing less than magical. Moss-covered old-growth trees lined the parkway. The mountains were mysterious and breathtaking, and the steam rising off the water brought about a sense of ethereal intrigue.

The water in the Hoh River was low but dry gravel beds and monstrous dead trees strewn high on the banks spoke of a river that could become violent. Just a meandering trickle of a stream, on many occasions we had to get out of the raft and walk through shallow waters.

I was using a five-weight rod. Woolly buggers and weighted, colored wet flies were the order of the day. The river would be holding cutthroats and Dolly Vardens. An occasional spawned-out king salmon would be seen, and there were also a few summer-run steelhead in the river. I wanted the steelhead. But like all fishermen, I wouldn't say no to anything that tugged on my line. Within a few minutes, I landed a good-looking, light-colored, fourteen-inch Dolly. A fish right off the bat is always a good omen for the day. It keeps one's mind focused and alert.

[OPPOSITE] *Mornings are often quite cool on the Hoh. The Hoh is a glacier runoff river and the waters are usually glass clear but can be silted during the constant rains that occur in the area.*
[THIS PAGE] *The Hoh River is lined with old-growth trees. Elk are frequently seen grazing on grasses and eagles often swoop down to grab an unsuspecting trout.*

It was lighter in color than the ones I had chased in Alaska. It was also sleek, like a torpedo, not at all like the fat football fish I was used to.

The river was gorgeous, the water was clear and the massive trees and mountains witnessed to the remoteness of the area. We fished hard, changing flies often and pounding the banks and structure looking for fish. Throughout the day, I had hits from three steelhead and missed all of them. I did land several large Dollies, and near the end of the day Pat and I had fun catching a number of small "cuts" on dry flies.

That night, I soaked my sore body in the hot tub at the lodge again and had dinner with my family at the local Mexican restaurant.

In the morning we decided to return to the Hoh River. The other option had been to fish for salmon in a nearby stream. Honestly, I had caught so many salmon throughout the summer that catching more of these fish wasn't high on my list. I also didn't want to get involved with more combat fishing. So at first light we made our way to a higher section of the Hoh.

Once on the water, I landed a beautiful twenty-four-inch Dolly within a few casts, a good way to start the day. I thought at first it was a smaller steelhead, but I was not unhappy with the fish.

Around ten in the morning we were traveling in a heavily structured area full of huge fallen trees. Pat suggested casting over a fallen log. I cast the fly. The strike was instantaneous, a monstrous twenty-pound steelhead. I was momentarily thrilled. The hook was well set, and I had fresh knots and tippet on my line. But I knew I was in for trouble. We were going full steam downstream in a motorboat and the fish was traveling fast upstream on the other side of a log. This was not good. I had my drag set tight and the reel was reluctantly giving out line. This was a big fish.

The fish neared the roots of the tree, now at the opposite end of the log. The guide shouted for me to try to get the line over the roots but to no avail. The line tangled in the wood and snapped. The fish was gone. That was it.

I was disappointed. What could I say? That's just how it goes some days. There would be more steelhead, I told myself. I retied my line, attached another fly and went back to work.

But I sulked about it for a while. What did I do wrong? Should I have jumped out of the boat? Should I have tried to jump on the log? Should I have released the drag and let the fish run? I was quickly sinking into the LFS (Lost Fish Syndrome).

I had another slam on my line two hours later. It was a steelhead and another big one. I set the hook. I lost the fish. He was gone. I had now lost five steelhead in two days. I had also lost several cutthroats earlier that were either hitting short or just did not connect with the hook.

With childish drama I threw my pole in the water. I was done. It hit me like a sledgehammer. I had failed. Both my wife and my guide stood there laughing. For a few seconds, I regressed to something foreign in me. I like to think I have no temper. I don't throw my rod in the water. I don't behave that way. My father had a violent streak in him and I had completely rejected his way of living. I don't usually behave like him. But I just had. I wanted to think it was theatrics; I had an audience and thought I might as well entertain them. But some parts of my actions were true. I was, at that time, emotionally misdirected. My day was now ruined.

But things only went from bad to worse. Within a few minutes I was untangling my line while standing in deep water. I slipped off the disc on my reel and dropped it in the waist-deep water. The only way I could retrieve it was to pull all the line off the spool. Eventually, the backing appeared

and I was finally able to reassemble the reel, but then all the line tangled, and I succeeded in putting a deep cut in the middle of my new sixty-dollar fly line. To add insult to injury, my new rod broke at the ferrule. This was not my fault, but it was one more slap in the face.

Intellectually I realized that all of this was just part of fishing. This sort of thing happens to every one of us, it's not personal. All this is just minor stuff, I said to myself and tried to regroup. I continued fishing but my moodiness affected my fishing partners. No one spoke for quite a while. We all tried some halfhearted attempts at humor, but it wasn't time yet. Near the end of the day, I broke off several other flies as a result of bad casts, and I was happy to finally get off the water. Once we got back to the lodge and I'd had a little distance, I was finally able to laugh at myself. I thanked Pat Graham, my guide, paid him and complimented his guiding abilities. He had put me on fish, offered me tips on casting and, in general, showed me a great time. If I had failed to land a fish, that was my fault, not his. I will fish with him again.

That evening made up for my lousy day as we sat with Huckleberry Lodge owners Bill and Kitty Snelling. Bill has a major collection of exceptional antique fishing gear, including a set of original antique Leonard rods in mint condition. The set includes seven different poles ranging from a three-weight to a seven-weight. Over cocktails, Bill invited us to spend an extra night at his lodge. The following day he would be the host of the local Fish and Brew gathering and he wanted us there.

In the morning we checked out a few other local rivers and then attended the afternoon salmon party at the Huckleberry. The gathering is a legendary event. People come from Chicago and New York just to sample the numerous types of smoked salmon and home-brewed beer. Not only did a local bluegrass band entertain but also drummers from the Quileute tribe, one of the region's Native American tribes, entertained the gathering with vernacular songs and dances.

We finally made it to bed late at night. ⌒

October 17

THE STAMP RIVER

I live with
the constant fear
that my wife
will catch
more fish
than I do.

I had left Victoria the night before

and had found a motel room just north of Nanaimo on Vancouver Island. A spectacular place, the island boasts world-class fishing for trout and salmon of all species. My first forays into salmon fishing had been here on the island, when I was humiliated by my wife, who succeeded in landing eight great salmon while I caught nothing during our first week together. She has never let me forget it. When I go fishing without her, she says it's that I feel intimidated by her, that I live with the constant fear that she'll catch more fish than I do. And, alas, I hate to admit it, she often does.

At 5 a.m., I met guide Bill von Brendel at a parking lot just a few minutes from my hotel. We got along immediately. He's casual, has a sense of humor and is unassuming and chatty. We stopped on the drive up to the river and loaded up on high-calorie, high-cholesterol donuts and coffee.

The drive to the Ash River took more than an hour in the dark, but it was pleasant as the coffee had kicked in and we hadn't stopped talking the entire drive. We turned off the main road and onto a trail that would have been impossible for a mere mortal to find, and that, because of the potholes, brush and rocks that dominated the roadway, even a herd of llamas would have had a hard time trekking over.

These were virgin territories. There were no trail markers or signs to this section of the river. Few people had ever been there. Being part of the coastal rain forest, the brush was dense and rugged. Everything was covered with thick layers of dark green moss. The only footprints we found on the bank shores were those of elk, bear and otter. Trash or any other sign of "humanity" was not to be found. It was a place most fishermen only dream of visiting. Even better, to my astonishment, there were virtually no insects. Being a veteran Alaskan fisherman, I fully expected to be picked up and

[PAGE 171] *This beautiful three-foot steelhead was taken on a weighted black egg-sucking leech.*
[THIS PAGE] *Professional guide Bill von Brendel gets set to release a gorgeous fall steelhead taken on the Stamp River on Vancouver Island.*

Casting in the clear waters of the Stamp River in late
fall, one can expect to take trout, salmon or steelhead.

carried off by mosquitoes. But, thankfully, there were none.

Vancouver was in a drought and the water in the river was low, but what was there was perfectly clear. The bottoms of six-foot pools were as clear as the air before the discovery of fossil fuels. Huge boulders, perfect places for fish to hide behind during high waters, lined the riverbanks and protruded dangerously from the middle of the river, topped only with the mute of birds. Massive Douglas fir and aspen trees towered over the river, rendering a perpetual state of darkness to the setting. It was a place for druids and elves.

Bill was a true hunter of fish. He always spoke in a quiet voice and he approached the water with stealth and caution. He stared at the pools for what seemed an inordinate amount of time, spotting fish where I could not, and only on occasion did I see him wearing polarized glasses. Once in a long while he would "rock" a pool — toss a stone in the water to see if any fish scattered — after scanning it for quite some time. He would return later to fish once things calmed down.

That morning we hiked more than three miles upstream. It was exhausting. We climbed over massive dead trees, huge rocks and up and down treacherous cliff banks, each step made more precarious

because of everything's dense and slippery covering of moss and slime.

Bill's pace was relentless. He was a man obsessed with finding fish. He had fished the river four days earlier and had caught and released several large steelhead on dry flies. He knew they would be there; it was only a matter of time.

But all things change and not everything is perfect or the way we want it to be. In three hours we saw and caught no fish. Bill was more disappointed than I. After all, he was the guide and it was his job to lead me to the waters of plenty. Frankly, it would have been great to catch a few steelhead on dry flies, but searching for these fish is not like fishing for bass in Florida.

Steelhead are elusive fish. They are in the family of fish — called anadromous — that can swim from freshwater to saltwater and then back to freshwater again. Steelhead start their lives as rainbow trout in freshwater streams and rivers. At the end of their first year, they travel to the oceans and wander for a year or two. Then they return to the rivers of their hatching and spawn. Once they return from the ocean, they are called

[OPPOSITE, ABOVE] *Doing battle with large fish can stress equipment as well as the spirit.*

steelhead. Many of the adults survive and return again and again to the ocean. They come back to freshwater year after year, to bring life to new fish. They themselves may live several years, reproducing at their own calling on a yearly basis in fresh water.

By noon we were back at the vehicle. I was soaked with sweat. I hate to admit it, but I am no longer a young man. I was fully expecting to die of a heart attack on the riverbank. Finally, it was bright enough for me to see. The area was surrounded with majestic mountains, towering old-growth trees and the occasional clear-cut patch of land. Not at all pretty, these graveyards of tree stumps had been replanted and would, hopefully, regrow to thrill the spirits of generations that will come after us. We are all at fault for scars on the land. We all read books and newspapers, most of us live in homes made of wood and just about all of us use mountains of toilet paper yearly. Still, it saddened me to view the huge swatches of land completely denuded of the trees that were once homes to animals of all sorts. It takes three acres of mature trees to manufacture enough oxygen for one person to breathe. I hoped that we can curtail the cutting of trees before we run out of air. Without fanfare, we departed from the area.

Two hours later we arrived at the shores of the famous Stamp River. We were on a spot called General Money's Pool, a section of river made famous by one of Canada's fly-fishing legends, General Noel Money.

The river was perhaps forty yards wide, and the water was perfectly clear. It moved downstream at a class-one pace, no more than four feet deep in any of the pools. Massive trees lined the shores. There were still no bugs. The air was now about sixty degrees and the sun shined like ice cream on a hot day.

"Try this on for size," Bill said. He pointed to the dark, three-foot lines in the water. They were all salmon. An occasional light-colored ghost darted in and out of the schools. The light ones were steelhead — big ones.

Bill cast first. His pole bent and shook violently. He was forced to wander downstream to land the fish. Fifteen minutes later I photographed him holding a gorgeous thirty-inch steelhead. I was thrilled, and he more so!

Then I cast. And then I cast again and again and again. I changed flies and cast. I added

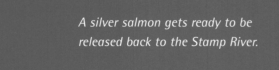
A silver salmon gets ready to be released back to the Stamp River.

weights. I changed lines to a sinking tip. I moved upstream and then downstream. I stood right next to Bill and followed his every move. I put on the exact fly he was using and cast. My "fish mojo" was not working. That afternoon he hooked sixteen fish. I caught nothing. To make matters worse, at least six other fishermen were in the two-hundred-yard area and each was catching fish one right after the other. I was sinking into serious depression.

It's hard to beat a guide on his home waters. But I just wanted one damn fish. That wasn't too much to ask. Bill "hand held" me through the drill. I did everything I was told to do. It was necessary to put the fly right in front of the nose of these fish. They simply would not move more than six inches to catch anything. The swing and depth of the fly had to be perfect.

Finally, near the end of the day, a coho grabbed my line. I battled him for fifteen minutes and was able to bring him to shore, where we made photos and finally released him to his home waters. I felt better.

Bill landed another beautiful steelhead and then a monster coho. We photographed both. But as a serious fisherman there is something humiliating about being fishless. There is something that fringes on shame when we are without a fish in front of others. There is something embarrassing about it. And we laughed about this as we drove home in the dark.

The following morning we again met in the dark. It was 4:30 a.m. and we took in more coffee and cholesterol from too many donuts. The ride to the river took three hours. I had no idea where I was. We parked on the side of the road, "wadered up" and wandered down a nearly nonexistent path to the stream.

This day was again to be steelhead on dry flies. Bill had been on this river several times before and had successfully landed numerous big fish with surface flies. He had called one of his buddies for a

MEOW MIX

My first foray into the realm of serious salmon fishing happened some fifteen years ago.

My good friend, artist Jack Gunter, called me from his home in Washington State and invited me to go salmon fishing with him and several other friends at Campbell River on Vancouver Island. I immediately accepted.

During this trip I caught six large kings and would drop my daily catch off at the local smokehouse. There they would be processed and canned and then sent to me at my home in Londonderry, New Hampshire. A week after I got home, four huge boxes containing one hundred cans of salmon arrived. As an animal-lover I often feed all kinds of critters. In this town two stray cats had adopted me, and I often fed them cans of cat food in the evening. One night I was out of my regular cat food, so I opened one of my smoked salmon cans and gave it to the appreciative kitties. In fact, this went on for several days and I found I had more and more cats visit me every night. Over time, I gave out more than fifty cans of my fresh-caught smoked salmon to these cats.

Then the Visa bill showed up. One hundred cans of smoked salmon cost me nearly a thousand dollars. There it was in black and white. Nearly ten dollars a can! And I had been feeding this stuff to the alley cats that were perfectly capable of finding and eating rodents for dinner. Salmon cat food was thirty-three cents per can in the grocery store but my smoked salmon costs me almost ten bucks a can! I felt like a fool!

The cats went hungry for the next week. But it was my own fault. After that, they were fed inexpensive, dry cat food. ■

report on the river the night before. Everything looked great, as he had been told.

But the stream waters, like the rivers south of us, had receded, and after nearly three hours of searching shallow pools and casting flies, no fish were found. I could see the disappointment in Bill's eyes. Good guides like to keep their clients happy. It's their job. Their very livelihood depends on it. And guides especially like to impress writers. Writers bring them significant business.

I am a firm believer in the idea that there is nobility in trying. There is no honor in not trying. Anyone can sit and watch reruns on TV or videos of people catching fish in Alaska. We gave it our best shot, and the fish and water didn't cooperate. That's how it goes. We could try other rivers in the area, but the water would be low in all of them. We made the decision to return to General Money's Pool. We knew there were fish there. It was only a three-hour drive, so what the heck!

Once there, Bill set about his way of catching a fish on just about every fifth cast. To this day I don't know how he did it. But I can say he's very good at what he does. Again, he walked me through the paces, and I again came up empty-handed. I did, however, learn a great deal from him.

At the end of the day, something large struck my line. Then I saw it roll. It was a huge steelhead. First up the river and then downstream it ran. I thought I would lose it as the line tangled briefly around my pole, but it held. I chased it all over the place. Finally, it calmed down and I brought it close to shore.

To my disappointment, it was foul hooked — the hook had pierced his dorsal fin. With a mighty tug, while he was still some twenty yards away, I dislodged the hook from his back and he swam slowly away. There is absolutely no honor in claiming a foul-hooked fish. It's far better to cleanly catch something you can be proud of. Taking foul-hooked fish is akin to cheating, and cheating only fools you. If you don't understand this, then you need to reconsider the very nature of your life.

Eventually, the sun set in the west and we made it back to our vehicle. We stopped for a burger before driving home. It had been dark for a while by the time I got back to my vehicle, and I was so tired I nearly slept in the car. Once back at the motel room, I called my answering machine and checked e-mails, but I didn't answer any of them. They could all wait.

If you want a really great experience, check out steelhead on dry flies at just about any time of the year. Be sure to call Bill von Brendel in Nanaimo. He's the best! But make sure there's water in the rivers before you go.

October 19

IDAHO/MONTANA STEELHEAD

All day long
I kept hearing,
"You should
have been
here yesterday."

We had dropped Tina off at the airport in Seattle

the day before and had driven east toward the Rocky Mountains for most of the day, spending the night in Coeur d'Alene, Idaho.

The next morning we continued making our way east, but by nine we were hungry and pulled off I-90. We aren't ones to eat at fast-food restaurants; we like down and dirty places with real food. We found a great-looking, seedy sort of a place in an industrial section of a blue-collar mountain town, a small, out-of-the-way place with a sign reading "CAFE." Below the sign was another that said "Bible study, 7 p.m., Thursdays." Yet another off to the side read "Open season on Terrorists. Licenses Sold Here" and below it, "Defeat Terrorism. Get us Out of the UN." We really didn't know what to expect inside but the folk art quality was quite evident. Besides, we were only out for breakfast and it's tough to ruin pancakes or eggs. The quality of the food would speak for itself. Regardless of the politics, I knew this could be an interesting meal.

Once inside, I realized that this was certainly one of the most interesting and yet confusing places I had ever been. Printed on the place mats for each setting was the Lord's Prayer. The Ten Commandments were neatly printed on several large signs throughout the interior of the building. Bumper stickers plastered the walls with religious slogans. "Respect the Sanctity of Life" was one of the more prominent ones. This was a serious place.

Above each of the bathroom doors read "For Customer Use Only. All Others Pay 50 Cents Per Use." Political pamphlets on the wall were ultra-right wing and supported the efforts of a local candidate to "throw out the rascals and incompetents in Washington" and "return all power to the states and communities." "Get out of our lives" was the politician's war cry. I'm certain that he has many followers in this part of the country. Other signs in the building read "This Country is Led by Environmental Communists."

In another corner of the room stood a video game where one could blast terrorists. Or you just might pass out from the "extraordinary G-forces while piloting a supersonic fighter plane doing battle against the forces of evil!" Although Lindsey was intrigued by the game, I opted out of the opportunity to render death and destruction to the hearts and lives of those whose lifestyles differ from ours.

The restaurant seated maybe twenty people in all. We found a table and chairs in the far corner of the room. Another family was just finishing their breakfast. After giving us the "once over," they politely said good morning. We returned their greetings.

After we had waited for more than a half hour, the waitress announced that she needed something from the store, took out her car keys and drove off! By this time my family and I were the only ones in the restaurant. She was gone for almost twenty minutes and finally returned with a bag of ice in her hands. I frankly don't know what I would have done if other customers had come in.

After almost an hour of waiting, she finally arrived with our food. It was exactly what we had ordered and we ate our fill, asked for our check and paid the bill. Just before we left the waitress took me by the arm and showed me the slot machines in the back room. "Best damned slot machines in the whole county!" she said. I believed her.

Just a block down from the restaurant was a large barn with horses in the front corral. A sign at

[OPPOSITE] *Trout taken on dry flies on Silver Creek.*

the entrance to the stable read "BREEDING LESSONS." We left town not knowing what to think.

Back on I-90 East, we began to cut back and forth across the Clark Fork River. A majestic vein of water, this river, like most of the rivers and reservoirs in the Northwest this year, was low. But it had great character and no doubt held fish. Without my saying a word, Michele looked at me and said, "Go ahead!" I didn't argue. At the next five turnoffs I managed to throw a few flies and test the waters. But, alas, no luck.

At this point I should now mention another syndrome well recorded and documented in the annals of fishing psychobabble. It's called the "IDC" syndrome. It stands for "I Don't Care." It's a serious concern. It happens like this: Once someone has lost several fish over an extended period of time or has caught absolutely nothing when everyone else is catching fish, a serious mental laissez-faire attitude sets in. The fisherman actually stops caring about fishing. He casts with a poor attitude, doesn't pay attention to any fishing details, doesn't concentrate, doesn't set the hook properly, ties knots incorrectly and uses stupid and incorrect flies. In short, he is a defeated man.

The above describes me perfectly at this time.

[OPPOSITE] *Known for magnificent scenery, the Salmon River and surrounding wilderness area can tantalize any fisherman. Lewis and Clark camped near the river and ventured down the extraordinary valleys and waters.*
[BELOW] *A small trout being gently released back to the Salmon River.*

I had taken very few fish during my past several outings. Everyone else was catching boatloads of fish, but I just couldn't get into it. I considered taking up bowling.

But the scenery was beautiful. Michele and Lindsey played on the shores . . . and I knew that things could get a lot worse. I resolved to either get help from a therapist or approach fishing with a better attitude.

Eventually, we found another road and made our way down toward North Fork, Idaho, where we were about to spend several days fishing on the famous Salmon River for steelhead.

At one point as we traveled, I couldn't help but notice off to my right a building with a sign: "Fly Shop Now Open!" How could I resist? Once inside, Michele and Lindsey entertained themselves playing with the owner's hunting dog. I, of course, was talked into purchasing several new flies that were guaranteed to catch fish on the Bitter Root River that ran along the highway. Another symptom of IDC: the one who suffers from it can be talked into anything. That's why I bought the new flies instead of a bowling ball.

In time we made our way to the boat launch, where I was told great fishing could be had from shore. Within fifteen minutes I was in waders and ready to go!

The water was clear and the bottom rocky. The shores were lined with massive dead trees, washed down from the mountains by waters that, no doubt, could be torrential. I cast first under a bridge. No luck. I moved downstream and cast up against a few logs. No fish. So I wandered across the river to fish the opposite shore. First cast and a strike — a great-looking fourteen-inch rainbow. I was thrilled. A few more casts and then another fish and then another. I was on a roll. I didn't take anything big, but it was just great fishing. Within an hour, I took five nice rainbows.

Then it stopped. I cast and recast. I had been throwing a large hopper with a bead-head prince nymph attached to the end fly and had caught all my fish on the nymph. As darkness approached, I looked closely at the flies I was using. The hook had broken off the nymph. That's why I had ceased catching fish. I had felt that I had been hit by numerous fish in the last half hour but just couldn't get them on the line. I now knew why.

But my mental chaos had lifted. I was a new man. Gone was the trauma of fishing. I had confidence in myself again.

We arrived at the Hundred Acre Wood, a B&B resort in North Fork, Idaho, late that night. We would spend the next four days fly-fishing for the mighty steelhead on the famous Salmon River. Also known as the River of No Return, it boasts an impressive run of steelhead surrounded by the most spectacular scenery in North America. It is a place of high drama, stunning mountainous cliffs and herds of wildlife, including elk, bighorn sheep, deer and other game.

OCTOBER 20 We had breakfast at the B&B. Afterward, I fished the pond in the back of the complex. In the past it had been a fish on almost every cast, but the cool weather has set in and knocked the fish down. They would hit neither my dry or wet flies. Lindsey entertained herself by feeding the geese and ducks that followed her around the yard. After a while, the ducks got too aggressive and started nipping her shoes and fingers. I had to rescue her from the onslaught of feathered creatures. Once she ran out of bread, however, she took to feeding the llamas. She particularly liked their soft noses.

Later, we drove down to the Salmon River. It was as beautiful as I remembered it, my first experience here had netted me five good-sized steelhead in a single outing years earlier. The only difference this time was that there were significantly more fishermen. Nonetheless, we were still there early in the season. There were plenty of fish in the river, but the main run would not be for another two to three weeks. Once the main run began, the combat fishing would rival that of the Kenai River in Alaska during the sockeye salmon season. I had no desire to experience that again.

We drove the length of the river that was accessible by car. In the seasonal town of Shoup (population 4) we had lunch — including the greatest milkshakes in the world. After lunch, we stopped at several sites on the river and tried our luck. Initially, I used a sinking black egg-sucking leech, then switched to a large floating hopper with an added nymph. No luck at any of the four or five places we tried. One gentleman standing near me succeeded in landing a thirty-inch steelhead. I made photos of him and his fish before he released it back into the wild. The Fish and Game people were out in full force and everyone traveling the road had to stop and be checked for fish, so it was late when we finally got to bed. I dreamed of catching a monster steelhead. But dreams, unfortunately, are not reality.

OCTOBER 21 It's now evening. We had dinner at the gas station. I'm certain I'll have indigestion for the rest of the week.

I'm taking up bowling when I get back to New York. I'm going to get a sixteen-pound ball and a bowling shirt with my name emblazoned above the pocket and join a league and knock down all the pins I can. I can't catch any fish, so I might as well try an activity that doesn't cost so much or require so much traveling.

I had hired guide Ed Link to fish me on the Salmon River. According to the other guides and fishermen I met, people were catching three to four steelhead per day, big fish averaging in the thirty-two-inch range. Fishing was good, I was told.

Ed is a living legend in these parts. He's guided the Salmon River for the past twenty-nine years and knows the waters better than anyone. Even the fish and game officers acknowledged that he was the best. So how could I lose?

We met at around nine in the morning, put in the boat and then did the shuttle ourselves, using Ed's truck to deliver the van. Finally, we were off. Ed is the most meticulous and patient man I've ever met. He attends to every detail and patiently fishes a hole until he is certain that there are no fish hanging around anywhere (and that can go on for hours). He is almost obsessive about mending the line properly. Knots, casts, approach to the holes, position on the holes: everything must be right. Even the lunch was exceptional. He served filet mignon wrapped in bacon, baked potatoes with sour cream, onions with a special hot sauce and then finished the lunch off with apple pie with whipped cream, cooking everything (except the pie) right there on the boat! It was the best lunch I've ever had! Equally important, he is a genuinely great guy!

I encourage just about every guide I have employed to fish with me. I learn an enormous amount from watching professionals fish.

Besides, two poles are better than one and when I need fish photos, who better to ask than the pros on their own water?

So we fished and fished and then we fished some more. When I fish, I actually fish. This may seem like a strange statement but many people will fish for a while, chat with their guides or cohorts, look at the scenery, take a nap or drink cocktails. But I fish the entire day. I'm not there to relax. I find that the art for me is tying the knots, casting the flies and hunting for the fish. I feel good about myself when I'm doing something productive. Why waste time?

But today we caught no fish. No matter what we did, the fish wouldn't bite. I enjoyed Ed's company a great deal and learned an enormous amount from his ability to fish and teach, though; I would use my newly learned skills throughout the rest of my life. But to be realistic, fishing for steelhead is, at best, difficult. Although there are plenty of fish in the water, the fish and game officers have interviewed everyone on the river and calculated that this week it is taking about forty-eight hours of fishing for one person to land a steelhead.

OCTOBER 22 It's now a little after four in the morning. I am thinking about yesterday. Bowling or shooting pool the rest of my life sounds better and better.

Michele and I had arranged to fish with guide Chris Swersey of Silver Cloud Expeditions. He, too, is a long-time guide and capable fisherman. Before we met him, we left Lindsey at the local baby-sitter's home. When I went in to introduce myself to the sitter, her small, hairy schnauzer came up and bit my leg. This was not good. If he had bitten through my expensive new waders, I would have shot him. But his teeth didn't puncture the material. Fortunately, the dog calmed down and immediately took to my daughter. They were inseparable throughout the day.

The days here in Idaho begin at around twenty degrees in the early a.m. and they generally climb to about fifty in the daytime. The water temperature is around forty, so standing in water all day long can put a serious chill on you. We wore all kinds of layers of clothes.

We fished a different section of the river, today, the fall colors along the river dazzling us with their brilliance. Chris had all his high-quality equipment ready and numerous poles rigged; he knew how to use the gear. He also knew the river exceptionally well, rowed like a pro and was on time. What more can a client ask? Fish would be nice, but a guide has no control over their appetites or aggressiveness.

The more we understand the psyches of those involved in the fishing experience, the more meaningful and wondrous our own lives become. So far I've only mentioned psychological problems as they relate to fishermen. But guides have a far more difficult job than one can ever imagine. When things go wrong, they always resort to the "YSHBHY" explanation – "You Should Have Been Here Yesterday!"

All guides say this. This is not specific to one region or group of guides. It's written in their genetic codes. They say this because the fishing is lousy, which just about sums up the fishing on the Salmon for the past three days.

In the early morning we pulled plugs in a method called back drifting. We also tried numerous fly-fishing techniques, including dries, wets, and nymph fishing. I even lowered myself to using a spinning rod and threw spoons often throughout the day. No luck.

Now I realize that steelhead are elusive fish. When the bite is off, you might as well forget it. But you can't catch a fish if your fly isn't in the water. And all day long I kept hearing, "You should have been here yesterday."

As the sun set, Michele was shivering as I took my last few long casts, reflecting on the idea that fishing is about the good old outdoors: sunrises and sunsets. It's about good times with friends and getting to renew old friendships and make new ones. It's about time away from work and the joy of learning new skills. It's about rejuvenating and refreshing oneself.

But then I thought, "How mental have I become?"

Nuts to all the head stuff. I just want a steelhead. Just let me catch a fish, please. I've worked for it. I deserve it. All I want is just one wild fish. I don't want to hurt it. I just want to give it a little two-minute nightmare and then release it back to its home. That doesn't seem too much to ask.

As Chris and I finalized our arrangements for fishing the next day, we parted with the ultimate words of wisdom from our guide, "You should have been here yesterday!"

[THIS PAGE] *Although the Salmon River sees its fair share of fishermen, individuals can almost always find a magnificent cove all to themselves.* [OVERLEAF] *The bautiful Salmon River.*

Steelhead fishing is more difficult than fishing for muskies with a broomstick fishing pole or bone fishing under the hot sun. Steelhead fishing is just hard work. I had been spoiled by my earlier steelhead adventures, where I had caught at least five every other time I had fished for these guys. I thought I was a great fisherman, but I have been brought back down to earth. I am a humble man now, trying to maintain a sense of self-respect and dignity — but it's hard.

OCTOBER 23 It's nearly five in the morning and I have prayed to the great fish gods in the sky. I apologized for cursing too much. I said I was sorry for not doing my homework in grade school. I apologized for calling my high school biology teacher a lousy teacher. I said I was sorry for everything I had ever done wrong. I promised to work harder in the future. Please, O Great Fish God, let me catch a big fish. I promise to become a better person if you will just let me catch one steelhead.

It's now 8 p.m. and I have caught nothing all day. Nothing at all. I will admit to foul hooking a disgusting sucker, but that's it. I tried hard throughout the day. I threw black and purple leeches. I tossed feathered muddlers, streamers of all colors, tarpon flies and just about everything else I could find in my tackle bag. I even threw spoons again on a spinning rod. We hit every hole and fished till I was blue in the face. As I write this, I'm exhausted. My shoulders ache, the joints in my hands are sore and my feet are still numb from standing in forty-degree water all day. We finally got off the water at around 6:30 p.m. My family and I drove down to the local diner where we had dinner and spoke with several of the fishing guides.

"Should have been here last week," was all they said. God help me.

OCTOBER 25 We arrived in Ketchum, Idaho, two days ago. The drive from North Fork, Idaho, was stunning. Arguably one of the most beautiful drives in the country, the highway follows the banks of the Salmon River and passes through the Salmon-Challis National Forest and the Sawtooth National Recreation Area. We stopped frequently along the shores of the river to gaze at the late autumn colors of the towering cottonwood trees that dominated in the region.

Lewis and Clark camped here and followed the river hoping to get to the Pacific Ocean. Deer and elk were everywhere. Bighorn sheep crossed the highway. As we drove through tiny communities we wondered, as all travelers do, "What do these people do for a living out here?"

When we arrived at Ketchum near evening, we met our old friends Doug and Janis Tedrow. Doug, one of the finest rustic furniture makers in the country, introduced me to Jerry Ring, owner of Silver Creek Outfitters. Dedicated to advancing the art of fly-fishing, Silver Creek Outfitters offers numerous classes in fly-fishing, including courses just for women and kids. They also guide trips not just around Ketchum, but throughout the world as well, and their store rivals any in the country. When Jerry offered to have one of his guides take me fishing in the morning, I accepted immediately.

Guide Dave Huber met me at the store around 10 a.m. "No reason to go out any earlier," he said, "the fish won't bite until the first hatch, which is usually around midday." From the store, we drove down to Silver Creek, about an hour south of Ketchum.

Known for impressive runs of huge steelhead, the fall season brings out hundreds of fishermen to try their luck. Taken on a woolly bugger and an eight-weight rod, this steelhead was released back to the water.

A fisherman casts to the quiet waters of Silver Creek.

This was the land of Ernest Hemmingway; deer, ducks and upland game birds everywhere and the clear spring waters of Silver Creek full of huge trout. Although Hemmingway spent an enormous amount of time in the area, he is known to have fished here only once. He was far more interested in bird hunting. Most of the river we were on is privately held and is clearly posted with "no trespassing" signs. The waters open to average folks are owned and maintained by the Nature Conservancy. After we signed in at the outpost station, we drove along the river for quite some time just looking. We saw no fish rising.

I have fished with dozens of guides around the country. Each has his or her own distinct way of leading trips and fishing their waters. Dave's approach was as unique as any I have ever experienced. Once we found our way to the waters, we spent an inordinate amount of time watching for rising fish and waiting for a hatch of some sort to tell us what the fish would be eating. According to Dave, absolutely nothing happens on this particular river that is out of the ordinary. If there are no hoppers on land, then artificial hoppers on the water will simply not catch fish. Although I did not completely agree with him, I had learned a long time ago to do what the guide says.

However, I am also a firm believer in trying all sorts of things. If one pattern doesn't work, then try something else. Dave was adamant that the fish in this river had seen everything ever conceived of by the human race and would only strike what was seasonally and environmentally correct. So our approach to this river was purely academic. Over time our method proved ineffective. The fish just wouldn't take our flies. Although I argued that we should try other approaches, Dave felt that we had a much better chance of landing something big on the nearby Big Wood River.

Fishermen, beware: If you want to play with the big boys, you have to be prepared. You can approach fly-fishing as a recreational sport or you can elevate the activity to an intellectual art form. Sure, there is the graceful and beautiful act of throwing the fly, but that's only the beginning. If you want to catch fish, it's critical to fully understand the bugs that fish eat and when they eat them. Without going on and on about this, it's necessary to comprehend the differences between a *Callibaetis* hatch and a mayfly, duns of all sorts and the incredibly subtle differences between emerging and "ready to go" bugs of all kinds. If you want to catch fish, then do your homework. Understanding entomology is the key to being more than just another "hacker" on the river.

Once we arrived at the Big Wood River, we wandered down into an unassuming hole in the stream. No more than a few feet deep, the water was partially obscured by fallen leaves . . . but there were fish there! My gut reaction was to throw black woolly buggers or leeches at them. Dave's approach was different. He chose size-eighteen and -twenty nymphs. Flies this size defy the comprehension of the average human. Once it's cast into the water, you can't see the fly if your life depended on it, and once the fish hit the fly, setting the hook is nearly impossible. These tiny hooks are easily pulled out of the mouths of the fish. And even of you are lucky enough to get a fish, the line is so small that it can easily be broken if the fish runs into the rapids or if an unwary fisherman decides to muscle in the fish.

But we did catch a few fish — nothing huge. I landed and photographed a nice rainbow, then released it. We missed a few others, but all in all, the day was quite successful. Although we didn't catch as many fish as I would have liked, I saw some glorious new waters and learned new approaches to different fishing situations.

There is time for one more psychological fishing phenomenon. It's called the "ITSWCXF" affliction. It almost always affects guides, but it also affects just about everyone who has fished more than once in his/her life. It's the "In This Spot We Caught X (any amount will do) Fish" affliction. I've heard this so many times I can't take it anymore. In the same vein, my father used to say, "This is the spot, fellas." Guides always say this. I don't know if it's bragging or the guide just wants you to know there really are fish there. Probably it is to ease the concerns of clients not catching any fish. If, however,

I am not catching any fish in a spot where I have been told that on the previous day a hundred fish were taken, I want to either throw up or kill myself because I am obviously too incompetent to catch any of the fish the guide has assured me are there. Guides should be more sensitive to how insecure many of us wanna-be fishermen really are.

OCTOBER 26 I'm a stubborn guy; I don't give up easily. After breakfast, I took Michele and Lindsey down to Silver Creek to the same spot where I had fished the day before. "Just a few casts," I said, and into the creek I wandered. Six hours later, we left the river.

So I put on my bifocals and tied a size-eighteen mahogany baetis of some sort onto my six X tippet and away I went. Although I knew fish were there, they were reluctant to hit my flies. I changed flies many times, but fish only rose to my offerings twice. Unfortunately, I failed to hook either of them.

But in truth I enjoyed myself throughout the day. It was comforting to have my family with me. They seemed to enjoy themselves playing games, picking weeds, following insects and marveling at the scenery. Silver Creek is a spectacular river, a national treasure.

Later in the day, I wandered upstream and waded for more than a few miles down the middle of the river, throwing flies at trophy-size fish that had interest only in their world and not mine. The deep, dark holes, perfect structure, and undercut banks were ideally suited for fish and fly-fishing. The water was so clear, it almost seemed invisible. I could see every detail on the floor of the river fifty yards away.

I took some comfort knowing that no one else on the river had caught anything that day either. In fact, few fish had been taken on the river in quite some time. Other fishermen we met speculated on the water's low productivity. Reasons ranged from the full moon, to the drought and low water, to the pressure of too many fishermen and on and on. Here's the real answer: sometimes they bite and sometimes they don't.

There are a few different approaches to fly-fishing. One can partake in the activity and view it as a subsistence activity. If necessary, the fish we catch can sustain us. Trout do make excellent meals. But as the individual grows within the sport, fly-fishing becomes more, a profound art form. The casting of a fly is a beautiful dance and a fluid human movement that can take years to master. Anyone who has acquired the basics of casting and then gone on to be able to complete casts with great precision and accuracy can sense the artistic skill growing within them.

Art is a verb. It is a process. Art is not passive. It does not hang on walls. The great art in museums, although stationary objects, moves one's mind to new heights. Fly-fishing can do this as well.

I marvel at the creative capacity in humans. We have a tendency to make things extraordinarily complicated. Check out the almost infinite variations of flies offered in a professional fly shop, for example. As a side note, you should know that fishing with dry flies is a hundred times more difficult than fishing with wet flies. Dry fly-fishing is pure science. There is no luck to it. But fly-fishing encourages creativity in humans. The great fly fishermen have an almost infinite knowledge of the fish and their environment. At the same time, they are generally successful in their personal and professional lives.

I love fly-fishing gear. The act of tying tiny knots on very thin line can be mesmerizing. The entire world stops when I'm standing in a river, waist deep, tying on a new leader and fly. Nothing else exists. Nothing else matters. For me, it is a good thing. Fly-fishing doesn't just happen, it takes time. It's not at all like taking a bamboo pole with a worm, hook and bobber and fishing for bluegills. Fly-fishing requires enormous energy. It requires great thought and persistence. It's not for everyone.

It would be easy to sit in front of a fire and watch football games on TV on our days off work. It would be easy to go to movies or take naps all day. But some of us seek challenges. Some of us seek a connection with our human heritage that is not available or accessible through media and technology. For millions of generations, we lived in caves and trees. We had our spears and arrows and fishing gear at our sides at all times. In the evenings, we sat around a fire and talked of our adventures of the day. The art of conversation was probably more developed during those times than it is today.

As we evolved, our complicated world and our amazing technology took us away from where we came. We lost contact with the real world and distanced ourselves from our roots. But every now and then we hear the calls of the wild and must return to the wilderness from which we came. The trees and the water beckon to us. The wind plays its magical music to us. A fish on the end of our

lines reminds us that we could survive in the wilderness if we needed to.

So, many of us need the wilderness, the trees, the fishing. The quality of our lives is improved and we feel more comfortable with ourselves when we partake in wilderness activities. We need to do more of it.

OCTOBER 28 It's now after ten in the evening. We are in a hotel in Ontario, Oregon. Around eight in the morning my friend Doug Tedrow suggested that we spend the day with an employee of his, Jack Meriweather. A calm, unassuming man in his sixties, Jack exudes a level of confidence that immediately draws people to him. I didn't take long to answer his invitation to go fly-fishing.

About eleven in the morning, we met Jack and wandered off to fish the Big Wood River just south of Ketchum. In this area, Silver Creek receives all the attention and the Big Wood is seen by most visiting fishermen as a trickle of water not worthy of consideration. All I can say is, boy, are they wrong!

Today I not only learned certain things about fly-fishing, but I also succeeded in making a fool of myself. The river is no more than twenty yards across at any given point. There are a few deep holes but the river runs about four feet at its deepest point. I wandered in and began fishing in the style I felt was appropriate for the river: I wandered along the edges throwing long casts into seams in the center of the river, initially using hoppers. I was wrong on all counts.

Jack took me aside and explained the river to me, a profound and humbling lesson. The fish were not in the middle, he told me, but rather, they were in the calm water on the very edges. They hit his flies — specifically, olive brown number-sixteen caddis flies — in about six inches of water. He wandered straight up the middle of the river and never cast more than six feet. His casts resulted in perfect drifts with no drag on the flies as they floated down the river. He easily caught twenty fish. I caught only one. But I understood and learned my lesson.

Jack fished with a mint-condition, eight-foot bamboo fly rod that his parents had purchased for him in England in 1954. Unfortunately, I struggled throughout the day with my gear. The felt had worn off my wading boots and I took two serious falls while walking on the rocks in the river. I also slipped several other times and nearly killed myself. I didn't have my glasses with me and fumbled with building a complete new leader.

Know your rivers, the fish, and their habits and you'll catch fish. Without the knowledge, forget it.

[OPPOSITE] *Certainly one of the classic western rivers is the Silver Creek. Flowing through Nature Conservancy land south of Ketchum, Idaho, the river allows easy access for the fisherman. A technically challenging river, its fish have seen just about every fly ever conceived of by the human race.*

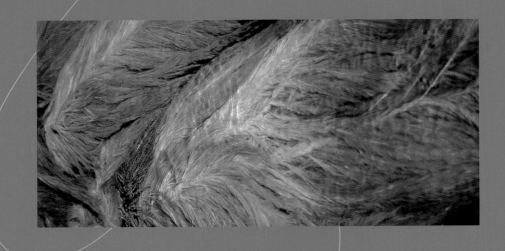

November 5

LEE'S FERRY, ARIZONA

"Howdy, son, we sure do like your doll and purse." The cowboys broke into laughter.

Two days ago, I was to leave for Arizona,

my airline ticket purchased and paid for in full. That evening, though, Michele and Lindsey came to me saying that I was gone too much and that they missed me. Lindsey, with tears in her eyes, said she wanted to come with me. What could I say?

So I hurriedly got three new tickets off the Internet before I realized that I had just lost $677 because I could not change or reuse my first ticket. So be it. On the one hand, it seemed so foolish to buy the new tickets — I could have bought myself a new high-end fly rod with the money I had lost. On the other hand, any father who cannot comfort his young daughter is not worth his salt as a parent, and the thrill of having my family along far outweighs any new toy I might acquire. I resolved to not think about it again.

So we packed our bags and left for the airport. The security officers chose us for a random check. We had to completely unpack our bags and explain to a non-English-speaking, non-fishing agent exactly what all our fishing gear was about. It took so much time, we nearly missed our flight.

But we finally arrived in Phoenix and spent the night at my in-laws'. We were able to depart for Lee's Ferry and fishing three days later. We drove most of the way there in the dark, and I'm sorry to say that we missed some of the most spectacular scenery in the world, but we would see it on our return trip.

[PAGE 198] *A view of the Colorado River as it snakes its way through the Grand Canyon.*
[OPPOSITE] *A small trout caught on a dry fly is about to reenter the water.*
[THIS PAGE] *Casting a fly in the Colorado River below Lake Powell.*

Casting to the gentle waters of the Colorado, a fly fisherman stands silhouetted in the shadows of the Grand Canyon.

At this point, I have to admit something: I am a fly-fishing addict. It's a problem. I think about fishing all the time. I have far more gear than I can ever use and I have driven several charge cards to their limits with my incessant fishing trips. I'm certain that my business is suffering because of my absence, and I know that my family misses me a great deal when I'm gone, stressing my relationships with them.

But I do have a plan. As a businessperson I know that I can somehow profit from all this. Since I'm certain that others suffer from the same addiction, I'll start a twelve-step program for fishing addicts! We could hold meetings once a week, where individuals would stand in front of the group and confront their addictions, the first step would be to admit that they have a problem and that they can't handle it by themselves. Actually, this is a very good business idea. I'm not going to discuss any more of it here because someone may take my idea and start the business before I do. Fishermen's Anonymous could be something great!

NOVEMBER 6 Finally, I met our guide that morning. Bill McBurney was a seasoned pro on the Colorado River. He had fished it for many years and had the right amount of experience and a large, enclosed, comfortable jet boat to insure that we would get the most possible chances for some great fishing.

We were staying at Lee's Ferry Lodge in Marble Canyon, Arizona, in the middle of absolutely nowhere. As we ate our breakfast, I couldn't help but notice the rather extended menu. Rattlesnakes, condors and coyotes run this place in the middle of the Arizona desert. Huge, dry mountains, sandy, hot desert and blinding sun are the only things in the area. I'm not kidding.

But the menu reads like something you would find in Aspen, Colorado. They offer over a hundred different kinds of beer as well an extended wine list. The service is great, the meals terrific, and the inexpensive rooms clean and comfortable. To top it off, the scenery is out of this world. This is definitely the place to stay when fishing Lee's Ferry.

So after getting a fishing license and traveling down to the river, we set off. The Colorado River is dam controlled. Completed in the 1950s, the Glen Canyon Dam controls the entire river and the surrounding valley. Before the dam was completed, the water was muddy and full of suckers, carp and other non-game fish. Once the dam was in operation, the river was stocked with trout. Cutthroats, rainbows and big brown trout inhabit the area today. Because different species of trout were introduced years ago, hybrid trout of all sorts have appeared, but all the fish I caught appeared healthy and were great fighters, and the dramatic colors on some of the rainbows I caught were not like anything I had ever seen.

In addition to the fishing, the scenery is dramatic; the river is lined with three-thousand-foot cliffs of huge red rocks that could humble any man. It is a place where peregrines can be seen hunting their prey, where condors soar on huge wings and where schools of trout can be seen "sipping" the river's surface as late-afternoon hatches of midges fall from the skies.

My first day fishing was casual. I'm told that first-timers to the river easily get caught up in the

scenery. I admit, I spent a significant amount of time just gazing into the cliffs that surrounded us. It was not like anything I had ever experienced. The fishing was productive. Most of the fish I caught were taken on small streamers with weighted line. We also took a number of rainbows on number-sixteen and -eighteen dry flies.

We had lunch on a sandy beach section of the shoreline. The setting was truly a photographer's dream, and I took photos throughout the day of my guide, Bill McBurney, and other fishermen casting their lines and holding fish. With the water so perfectly clear and no set of rapids so violent that it could not be fished, the day was over before it even began.

That evening after a wonderful dinner at Lee's Ferry Lodge, I suggested to Michele that she and Lindsey come fishing with me the following day. Although the Colorado is noted for its violent rapids, I assured them that the section of the river we would be on was completely safe. Besides, Bill's boat was large enough to accommodate many more people then just the four of us.

After breakfast the following morning, we made our way down to the boat landing and off we went. Lindsey gazed at the setting for just a few minutes and then said to me, "Daddy, this place is beautiful!"

We fished from the shores and the boat throughout the day, never bored and never stopping. We caught more fish than the day before, and they were larger. I was also thrilled to have my daughter reel in several nice-sized trout on my fly rod.

Bill proved to be a capable fisherman and a competent guide. He had significant knowledge of the area and was personable, professional and helpful. He could also tie the fastest knots of anyone I know. He is definitely the "go to" guy in the area.

Eventually, we said our good-byes and departed the area. The ride through northern Arizona and southern Utah was spectacular. We made our way to the south rim of the Grand Canyon and stood bewildered as we gazed, along with hundreds of other tourists, at the sights that nature provided before us. Vertigo overtook me and I had to find some solid ground to stand on.

Traveling back to Phoenix and the airport where we would catch our flight back to Lake George, New York, we made our way to the incredibly scenic town of Sedona. We stopped at the fly shop and

[OPPOSITE] *Lee's Ferry Lodge stands in the middle of nowhere. Blending perfectly with the surrounding mountains, the structure was created in classical western style. Boasting the largest selection of beer and the most-gourmet meals within a hundred miles, the facility also offers clean rooms and affordable prices! Just don't wander off during the night, as the coyotes and rattlesnakes just might get you!*

chatted with the owner about the Oak River. Though small and serene, the river is as picturesque as any and lined with indigenous red rock, whose color is brought out by the surrounding peak fall foliage.

The owner of the shop suggested that I use a short rod and nymphs for large brown trout spawning in the river, but we felt that we had too many miles to travel, and outside, the ominous dark clouds had started dumping serious rain and wind. Sadly (at least that's how my wife acted), we departed without fishing the river.

We also stopped in the small western town of Wickenburg. There we had lunch at the Frontier Restaurant in the old section of town. As we parked in the lot, Lindsey asked me to bring in her new doll so she could play with it while we waited for our meal. I picked up her new doll and the bag of accessories and went inside. Michele was putting Lindsey's shoes on her, so they were just a minute or so behind me. I walked into the front door and looked around. Inside were about fifteen cowboys, complete with chewing tobacco, cowboy hats and huge belt buckles. Everything went dead silent and all of them were looking directly at me. Suddenly, one of them spoke in a loud voice, "Howdy, son, we sure do like your doll and purse." The rest of the cowboys broke into uproarious laughter. Fortunately, just then Michele and Lindsey came in and we found a booth off to the side. "Don't you pay no attention to the boys here," the waitress told us when she came over. "They just like to give the tourists a hard time!"

I feel the need to proselytize here for just a few moments. Fisheries throughout North America are undergoing rapid change. Historically, many of the rivers I have fished were known to hold huge fish. In my conversations with many of the longtime guides on these rivers, as well as with state biologists, they report that many of the rivers are succumbing to the pressure of excessive fishing.

Fishing North American rivers isn't like it was twenty years ago. Many of the premier-grade rivers have been heavily fished and survive only because of stocking programs. Guides across the country have told me on many occasions that the days of catching a twenty-four-inch trout at every outing are gone. Without heavy stocking, East Coast rivers would be almost void of fish in just a few years. Even in my home region of the Adirondacks, premier-class rivers such as the Ausable and the Hudson are often void of native fish. Unfortunately, these rivers, like many other bodies of water, must be stocked to accommodate the pressure and demands from fishermen.

During the past few years, I have repeatedly heard cogent arguments concerning stocking programs. Some biologists have commented that stocking fish potentially alters the gene pool of the hatchery fish as well as native residents. The difficulty with such programs is the limited egg and sperm samples used in creating hatchlings. If every egg produced by a single fish is fertilized, hatched and then released into the wild, then the gene pool is ultimately severely limited. In order to maintain a healthy fish population, each fish in a normal, native, untouched fishery has to only reproduce one more fish. If only a few fish are chosen to reproduce, genetic defects can potentially dominate the setting, thus dramatically altering an entire species and fishery. With these thoughts in mind, serious consideration must be given to the future of stocking programs.

Other issues remain as well. In my earlier years, I often fished with a spinning rod and large artificial lures. I caught fish all the time and lots of them. But I noticed that the multiple treble hooks on these lures inflicted multiple wounds on the fish I caught. I have no doubt that my use of such lures killed many fish even though I released everything I caught back into the wild. Eventually, I removed the barbs on all the hooks and finally cut the treble hooks off the lures and fished with only one single hook on the lure. I no longer caught as many fish, but I felt more comfortable not inflicting so much carnage on the fish I did catch.

Each evening on the Colorado, as we wandered in and out of the fly shops, I couldn't help but notice the spin fishermen with their rods and their big treble hooks. Many of them commented on the fishing and mentioned that they had taken up to fifty fish in a day. I wondered how many they had killed or mortally injured with their large hooks.

Further, I often saw dead or dying fish floating past us as we fly-fished the river. These were, no doubt, carcasses of fish that had tangled with huge lures and paid the ultimate price. In short, as fishermen, we need to do whatever is necessary to preserve the resources that we cherish.

Moreover, fly-fishing has entered the mainstream. It's a trendy activity that has captured the imagination of millions. As a result, there are more fishermen on the rivers than ever before. I recall recently spending a day at a design project on the Beaver Kill River in Montana. The Beaver Kill is

[OPPOSITE] *Professional guide Bill McBurney of Ambassador Guide Service poses calmly before his boat just prior to a day's fishing on the Colorado River.*
[THIS PAGE] *Casting a fly in the Colorado River below Lake Powell.*

a small, dam-controlled stream no more than fifteen yards wide at any given point. One by one, the guide boats passed by me. Each boat had two fishermen and was separated from the other boats by just a few minutes. I must have seen a hundred boats that day. That goes on day after day all spring, summer and fall. Many rivers are like this.

Fortunately, during the past few decades, water quality has significantly improved in many places across North America. Nonetheless, significant problems remain. For one thing, a prolonged western drought has hampered many of the inland rivers. Because of global warming, this will continue to be a problem. We can only hope that our leaders find the wisdom and courage to address this problem.

Many of the rivers in North America are now catch and release only, and many sections of these same rivers are reserved exclusively for fly-fishing. Only artificial bait and barbless hooks are allowed. These rules help to preserve premier rivers.

Occasionally, draconian measures are taken to insure the health of rivers. For instance, state government has severely limited access to the Rogue River in northern Oregon. Even though numerous guides with boats utilize the river, fishermen without guides are only allowed to fish from the shore and not from the boats. This dramatically limits the amount of river that is fishable. State officials argue that the only reason the river remains healthy and the fish population remains high is because of these restrictions.

Regardless of the present laws, or regulations and restrictions that will be instituted in the future, we, as fishermen, need to act responsibly to insure the future of fly-fishing.

Sportsmen and conservationists need to act to preserve the rivers. Each of us should act in our own way to insure that our grandkids will enjoy the same experiences we have. Often, we rely on the government to solve these problems, and many times they act too late or incorrectly. We are capable of solving these problems ourselves. Let's hope that we do so.

[THIS PAGE-LEFT] *The author stands proudly, displaying a rainbow trout taken on a dry fly.*
[THIS PAGE-RIGHT] *An ideal hiding place for fishes of all kinds, the bottom of the Colorado River, upstream of Lee's Ferry, is complete with seaweed that dances to the gentle movement of flowing water.*

STONE FLIES ON THE BIG HOLE

We would
have to wait
another full year
for the return
of the big bugs.

The trip to Montana started out rocky. I missed
my 6 a.m. flight after having returned home only a few hours earlier at 3 a.m.
from a project in Connecticut, too tired to move. My wife, God bless her, drove
me to the airport for a later flight at 11 a.m. I had a ton of fishing gear, all my
camera stuff, a laptop and clothes for two weeks. I was exhausted. Unfortunately,
I was chosen for a random airport search and spent more than an hour explain-
ing the use of hook removers, pliers and fishing poles to an individual who was
far more comfortable at a bowling alley than in the outdoors.

[ABOVE] *Fishing on the Gallatin
River.*

[OPPOSITE] *Upper section of the Gallatin River.* [THIS PAGE] *Brown trout.*

Finally, I got on the plane. The first leg was a flight to Cincinnati, then another to Salt Lake City and then to Bozeman. As I relaxed in my chair I was happy to observe that the seat next to me was vacant. However, within a few minutes, a rather rotund person was escorted down the aisle and was soon filling the vacancy. "You stay right there and someone will pick you up when we land," said the flight attendant as she packed away the passenger's belongings. The individual now seated next to me simply said, "All right."

Her speech was slightly garbled and slurred, and though I could basically understand her, she was obviously mentally challenged.

"Do you like me?" she asked.

"You seem like a very nice person," I replied.

"Do you think I'm pretty?"

"You look very nice today," I said.

"I'm going to visit my aunt. Where are you going?"

"Well, I'm going to Montana for a while," I answered.

For the next two-and-a-half hours I answered every question ever conceived by the human race. Happily, the flight attendants were very appreciative of my efforts to both engage and entertain the individual next to me. First, they brought me champagne, then a dinner from the first-class cabin.

[THIS PAGE] *A fisherman enjoys the clear waters of the Gallatin.*

Each time my glass was empty they kindly refilled it.

We finally landed in Cincinnati. I said good-bye to my new friend and made my way to the next gate for the connection flight to Salt Lake City. Once on the plane, I stowed my gear and took my seat. I was exhausted and looking forward to a few hours of sleep. Within moments, however, an attendant escorted the same individual to the seat next to me.

"I'm so happy to see you," she said as she hugged me. "This is my boyfriend," she said loud enough for everyone in Cincinnati to hear.

For the duration of the three-hour flight, she continued chatting and squealing and laughing and gabbing about everything that had ever happened to her. These attendants also kept bringing me hot lunches and champagne. I am certain that I slept more than an hour during the flight and when I finally awoke my friend was still talking about anything and everything that came to her mind.

Once we landed in Salt Lake City my traveling partner was met by an escort. "I had the greatest time of my life," she said to me. She again hugged me and we waved good-bye as she was helped into a wheelchair. As I got off the plane, an attendant came over to me and said, "You're an absolute saint." I thanked her for the great lunches and the cocktails. I was certain I would have an enormous hangover in the morning.

The flight to Bozeman was uneventful. I slept all the way. When I woke I honestly didn't know where I was. Fortunately, all my luggage arrived with the flight and my rental car was ready and waiting. When I finally arrived in Big Sky at the cabin on the Gallatin River where I would be staying, I learned that the caretaker had forgotten to unlock the doors. I left a message on his answering machine and went for dinner. Upon my return, the cabin was still locked and all the hotel rooms in the immediate area were booked. That night I slept in the car in the driveway. In the morning I cleaned up in the cool, muddy waters of the Gallatin and headed back to Bozeman for a morning meeting. Painkillers and pancakes took care of my hangover and aching muscles. Maybe this seemingly jinxed trip would take a turn upward.

Three days later I met my good friend Keith Shorts from Jackson, Wyoming, to fish the Big Hole River, just out of Melrose, Montana. Keith was a professional fishing guide whom I had met years earlier. At around 8 p.m. we met at the Sunrise Fly Shop,

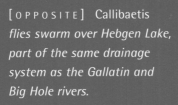
[OPPOSITE] *Callibaetis* *flies swarm over Hebgen Lake, part of the same drainage system as the Gallatin and Big Hole rivers.*

had a great dinner at the Hitching Post Diner and wandered over to the Big Hole Ranch, where we would be staying for the next three nights. The ranch is a world-class, private facility that occupies two and a half miles of riverfront. We were guests of the co-owners.

The second and third weeks of June are an absolutely fabulous time in the central region of Montana. That's when a major stone fly hatch occurs. It lasts for only a few days, so you have to catch it when it's just right. Stone flies are huge, monstrous creatures that are beloved by large brown and rainbow trout. Stone flies live underwater as tiny nymphs for three years. Then they morph into

flying insects and, in their last few days of life, mate and land on the water to lay their eggs. Soon they die and are gorged upon by ravenous underwater predators.

Nonetheless, anyone who has never spent time around stone flies, as I hadn't, is in for a treat. Early in the day I felt something crawling on my arm. I reached around and felt this hideous, monstrous bug crawling up toward my head. I shrieked and tore the insect from my arm while my cohorts laughed.

We had met our guide, Chuck Paige, at the Sunshine Fly Shop in Melrose. I had fished with him several times over the years and respected his ability to row a boat and catch fish. By 9 a.m. we were on the water. I was fishing a new four-piece, five-weight rod that handled perfectly. I had recently switched over to four-piece travel rods because cash-strapped airline companies had started charging me $75 to bring my standard two-piece rods along.

This trip was strictly dry-fly fishing. We threw huge stone flies (also occasionally called salmon flies) at all kinds of structures, close to the shores and into any fishy-looking place. The wind was strong but it was warm and the sun shone bright. My fast rod more than met the challenge of a windy day.

We didn't have to wait long. I knew for sure that my luck on this trip had changed when almost immediately I took a beautiful sixteen-inch brown trout. Then Keith landed a gorgeous rainbow and another large brown. On some sections of the river we would hook up with ten fish within a hundred yards. Other sections produced no fish at all. It astounded me that in the morning the fish would hit

flies dominated with red color, and in the afternoon they would only hit stone flies with purple or brown colors. But the fishing was good throughout the day; each of us probably tangled with a hundred or so fish. We caught nothing huge, but the day was graced by the capture and release of trout mostly in the fourteen- to twenty-two-inch range.

I had to chuckle to myself as I finally had the opportunity to fish with Keith. I had hired him on many occasions to guide my wife and me on Wyoming rivers. He is the consummate pro. But it was good to see him tangle his line a few times, get hung up on obstructions, throw a few poor casts and struggle with the wind as I did. It did my heart good to realize that fly-fishing is a complicated art and that all of us occasionally struggle with the mechanics of the sport.

At four in the afternoon we reached our take-out point. Though I realized that rowing a boat for seven hours in the wind had been strenuous, I was thrilled when Chuck suggested that we try another section of the river for the evening bite. So after shuttling the vehicles, we were again on the water.

This time the fishing was even better. Keith tried a number of different flies, including streamers and woolly buggers, but stone flies were the order of the day. We finally got off the water at 7 p.m.

That evening we had an absolutely delicious dinner at the Big Hole Ranch, a private, high-end facility that is one of the absolute gems of the fly-fishing world. We spent the entire evening telling and listening to fly-fishing stories.

The next day's fishing was superb. We started the trip higher up on the Big Hole River, and stone flies were everywhere completing the last cycle of their lives. I privately thanked them for their efforts. A friend in another boat counted 116 fish that came up to either hit or inspect his flies.

In the middle of the day we were struck with a violent thunderstorm that downed several trees and forced us to pull off the river. Fortunately, it lasted no more than a half hour and we were back on the water shortly. One right after the other, fish came to our flies.

Despite the weather, we did two more trips that day. The fishing was better in the evening. Toward the end of the day we had a great shore dinner and told more stories, sitting in the middle of a stand of weeds that was covered with thousands of creepy stone flies. For entertainment, we collected several flies, tossed them in the water and watched as predators from the deep immediately gobbled them up.

We spent time fishing the pond at the ranch the following morning. It contains a few hundred trout, many in the thirty-inch range. I caught a few and Keith caught several. The fish would only hit tiny, size-twenty elk-hair caddis flies.

Too soon, it was time for me to leave the ranch. I have to say that despite the uncertain way this trip had begun, by now I was unwilling for it to end. I drove down toward Dillon and found time to fish for a while on the famous Beaver Head Stream. That evening, I called my friends back at the ranch for a report on the day's fishing. Between four competent fishermen, only two fish had been taken the entire day. The hatch was over; fishing with stone flies was done for the year. We would have to wait another full year for the return of the big bugs.

The Big Hole River.

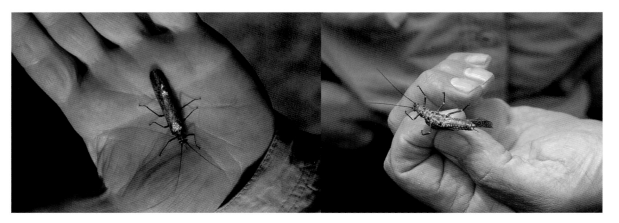

[THIS PAGE-TOP] *Casting on the smooth waters of Hebgen Lake.*
[THIS PAGE-BOTTOM] *Including their underwater nymph stage, stone flies have a lifespan of four years.*

*Chuck Paige fishing on
the Big Hole River.*

[THIS PAGE] *Fishing on the Gallatin River.*

A fisherman casts into the Gallatin River.

August 24

THE ALAGNAK RIVER

You look out for
your buddies
in a land
like this.

And so we were finally ready to depart

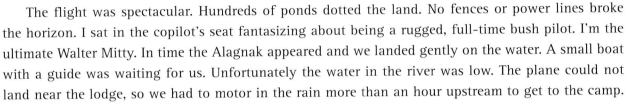

from King Salmon. Eventually our contact person showed up. The weather was preventing us from flying into the camp so all seven of us had lunch at Eddies in King Salmon, Alaska. The food was delicious. Around 2 p.m. the skies cleared enough to make traveling by bush plane possible. In time three of us were allowed to board an antique plane for a flight into the camp. The others would have to wait. The plane only held four people.

The flight was spectacular. Hundreds of ponds dotted the land. No fences or power lines broke the horizon. I sat in the copilot's seat fantasizing about being a rugged, full-time bush pilot. I'm the ultimate Walter Mitty. In time the Alagnak appeared and we landed gently on the water. A small boat with a guide was waiting for us. Unfortunately the water in the river was low. The plane could not land near the lodge, so we had to motor in the rain more than an hour upstream to get to the camp.

[THIS PAGE] *Harry Howard hooks a fish on the Alagnak River.*

It was a long cold ride. Beautiful and full of mystery, mind you, but a long, cold ride.

The camp was better than I expected. Several new wooden cabins housed clients, two people to a building. Flush toilets were out back and hot showers just off the kitchen. Each of the cabins had heat and electricity produced by a generator. The camp dogs — three gorgeous, well-trained blond Labs — greeted us all. They were critical to the setting; they chased the bears out of camp at night. I'm not kidding. The staff and guides were all professionals. Experienced men who had no fear and a profound respect for where they were interacted with my group as though we had been friends for years. The owner's wife and two young kids were also in camp. The two kids, five- and six-year-old girls, ran around barefoot for the entire summer catching fish and doing what little girls do. They were at home in the Alaskan wilderness.

We settled in. We were excited, about to spend a week in the interior of Alaska fishing for big fish. This was an area of Alaska where one does not wander off. Bears and wolves are everywhere. Flying over the land reinforced the notion of the pristine condition and ruthlessness of the region. This was a land for the physically and mentally able. All who ventured into the region took this place seriously. You look out for your buddies in land like this.

Once we had settled in, several of us pulled on our waders, rigged up our fly rods and wandered the hundred or so feet down to the river. The water was cold, about 45 degrees. Within minutes several of us had trout on our lines. Then someone landed a silver salmon, then another. The fishing proved to be excellent. We all started to relax from the flight. We fished without guides the first afternoon. Most of us knew what we were doing; only one of us was inexperienced. Throughout the week, however, each of us guests, besides the guides, spent time with him offering tips on everything related to fly-fishing. In a short time he could cast, tie knots and take fish from the waters with the best of us.

The days rolled by. I usually retired early to read and rest. Sometimes I'm less than social. That's just me. I also enjoy "messing" with my gear. Retying knots and arranging my tackle relaxes me. The others stayed up late playing cards, renewing friendships and doing what men do. We caught fish by the hundreds every day. These were strictly catch-and-release waters. We fished with barbless hooks. The guides recommended glow plugs and leeches. I used beads. I found I could land a fish every thirty seconds. Ten seconds to get one on the line and twenty seconds to reel him in. This went on for hours. Most were small ten-to-fourteen-inch fish. Fifty or so times a day I would land something between sixteen and twenty inches and ten times a day I would catch

something between twenty-two and twenty-six inches. Every day something huge would hit my line, but I never did manage to land an elusive thirty-inch trout. Nonetheless, I knew they were there.

These were not finesse waters. Tactics and fancy gear were not necessary. The fish were not leader shy. The butt section of a leader was forty-pound material. The tippet, usually twenty-pound test, was tied to that. Hooks and flies were tied to that end section.

Native trout in the area are called leopard trout. They are true rainbows but are covered with spots. They have a sleek body style, more like a torpedo then a fat football as the trout on other rivers in Alaska. They fought hard and ran and jumped with the best of them. There were more small trout than I expected. Nonetheless, small trout are signs of a healthy river. We also caught Dolly Vardens and Graylings by the hundreds. Graylings are the easiest to take off a hook; once in hand they immediately calm down. Dollies are "nut cakes." They twist and squirm and fight till the last second.

Trout are creatures of habit. For millions of years they have followed the seasons, feeding off what their environment produced for them. When the salmon are in, trout first feed on the eggs and then the fleshy parts of decaying salmon. They are "hard-wired" to do this. Good fishermen know this and fish accordingly. Many pros in the field swear that the colors and sizes of the beads we fish

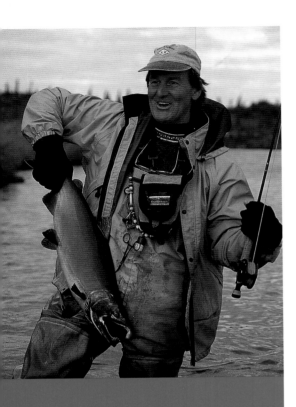

with must match the color and size of the salmon eggs that are in the waters. It's a good principle but I found this not to be true. I've caught trout on every size and every color of bead imaginable. If the trout are feeding, they'll hit anything. You just have to find the right spot where the fish are stacking up and you'll catch them.

We saw bears each day. On two occasions I had bears right outside my window at night. I know this because the dogs fearlessly charged the bears. The entire scenario is scary. First you hear rumbling and crashing ten feet outside your window. Then you hear the dogs charge and terrible growling. Moments later the dogs chase the bears through crashing trees. One does not wander out at night to enjoy the stars without first making lots of noise.

Each night we had fresh salmon appetizers. Dinner was usually a veritable feast. I usually ate only fish, but grilled steaks, prime rib and other delicacies were enjoyed by the others in camp. In the morning, hot showers were certainly welcome. In time my hands became swollen and sore. Cuts in my dry skin required numerous bandages. Once I returned from this trip to Alaska, I had to have several cortisone shots in my right hand to reduce the swelling. "Too much fishing", my doctor said. I did not take him seriously. I would return in a second and heal my wounds later.

One member in my group wandered off the riverbank and jumped a sleeping brown bear. Just fifteen feet away, the startled bear stood up on hind legs and snapped his jaws at Harry Howard. Harry yelled at him and the bear retreated into the woods. Harry was lucky to be alive. We picked him up in a boat fifteen minutes after the incident. He was white.

We had a comfortable week even though it rained every day. We saw the sun only once during the seven days we were there. It averaged about fifty degrees in the daytime — prime hypothermia weather. There were virtually no other fishermen other than us. Occasionally another boat would wander by, but we had the place — some fifty miles of river — to ourselves. High quality gear is necessary in a place like this. One just does not wander down to the local convenience store for more tackle or morning coffee. Gear must work correctly and you must know how to use it or you'll get into trouble. Further, one needs to be reasonably fit to fish wilderness waters.

The week was a success. We caught hundreds of fish each. We could not have had a better time. The guides were all competent professionals and the lodge was warm and comfortable. For a great time, check out Alaska Trophy Adventures. I'd go there again any day. In fact I wish I were there right now.

EPILOGUE

Fly-fishing
is not
about
catching
fish.

We pulled into the town of Island Park, Idaho.

Resting on the shores of the Henry's Fork River, the town is a strange assemblage of buildings and businesses that cater to the sportsman. We couldn't help but notice a number of fishermen standing knee-deep in the cool waters, casting flies. "If you want to, Ralph, go ahead." I have the greatest wife in the world. So we found a classy B&B and rented a room. Within fifteen minutes I was wading away, casting flies to fishy-looking places.

[OPPOSITE] *Drift fishing on the South Fork of the Snake River.*

The water was clear and rapid — not fast, mind you, but certainly moving along. I was startled at the evening baetis hatch. The flies, including PMDs, on the water were so thick one could almost walk across the river on them. When fishing with others one cannot help but notice if the other fishermen are catching anything. All the rods were straight. No fish were being taken. In time, as the sun went down, one by one, the other fishermen left the water to warm their bodies around a fire or at the dinner table. No one caught anything.

But as the sun sank farther, the fish turned on. Big fish started to gulp the surface. I could tell from the size of their tails that they were huge. Stalking or sight fishing for fish such as these requires patience, stealth and skill. This type of fishing is, no doubt, the most fun. I landed my dry flies directly upstream of the fish and carefully swung the line almost onto the nose of the rising fish. During the evening I had maybe five good strikes. But I was using size-eighteen PMDs. Each strike failed to connect to the tiny barbless hook that I was using. I caught no fish that evening.

Once on the shore, I met local guide Ernie. I never did learn his last name. We joked about how difficult it was to hook these fish. Henry's Fork is locally known as Humble Fork, as even the most skilled of fishermen often leave the water with no hook-ups and doubt and frustra-tion in their hearts. After dark we retired to the lodge where we shared a cocktail and talked about fishing.

The following morning I rose at 6 a.m. It was still pitch dark. Michele and Lindsey were still asleep. I donned a pair of long underwear, two pairs of socks and a pair of fleece pants. Over that, I pulled up my waders. On top, I wore two shirts, a wool overshirt, a fleece jacket and a lined raincoat. I walked out the door and nearly broke my neck on a patch of ice. I was fortunate not to have broken my rod in the fall. Nonetheless, within minutes I was at the water's edge. It was just daybreak. It would be another forty-five minutes before the sun showed its smiling face. A flock of geese honked in the background.

I watched the water for several minutes before I waded in. I wondered, if this is such a great river, why is no one else here? I saw no rising fish, there was no early morning hatch and the water was clear of any floating insects. I cast a few with a large hopper on my tippet. Just maybe I might get lucky. After three casts I had to put my rod down to remove the chunks of ice that had formed on each of the guides. Maybe I should just go back to bed, I thought. It would no doubt be much warmer. But, no, I stayed put and just enjoyed the setting. A moose wandered by on the opposite shore. He gazed at me for just a second and wandered off to do what bull moose do in the fall.

I tied a tiny Copper John onto the hook end of the hopper and made a cast. The line drifted perfectly down the middle of the river. The hopper disappeared, without creating swirls or splashes. It just went down. I lifted the rod. The line stuck. My pole shook. Line tore from my reel. The backing was now evident. I held the rod high. I could see only the tail of the fish. I didn't try to muscle him in. I was using a five tippet, a very light line for a large fish. The fish tore back and forth. I did not fight him. I let the pole do the work. The fish did not jump once.

I was in heaven. I just wished that someone were around to see this. I needed a net. I had none. Occasionally the fish came close and I could see its dark body. Once it got sight of me it showed all its strength and bolted again downstream. In time, it tired and I worked it near the shore. I took almost a half hour to land it. The fish was twenty-six inches. The largest trout I had ever taken in the lower forty-eight states, it was the epitome of health. Not a scar on it — it was as fat as a mature oak tree. I let it go. I giggled to myself. This was a once-in-a-lifetime fish for many people.

Ten minutes later, after I had removed significant blobs of ice from the guides and had re-tied my flies, I cast farther upstream. The fly floated gently past, some thirty feet from me. Again, the hopper disappeared. Moments later a huge rainbow danced on the water, perfectly hooked. I battled with it for twenty minutes before I landed it, removed the hook and sent it back to the home from which it came. It was twenty-four inches long and maybe eight pounds.

By now I was frozen. I had to de-ice my reel and line, which I knew had been damaged by the sharp edges of ice crystals. I wandered back up to my

room where my wife and daughter were dressed and waiting to be taken to breakfast. As I started to tell my wife of my morning, she pulled out the camcorder and insisted that I look at the viewer. To my absolute delight, she had recorded the complete capture of both fish. It was a good day and I must say that I looked pretty good landing the two largest fish I had caught in a long time!

I've just finished my last fishing trip before completing this book – Cody, Wyoming; Livingston, Montana and Henry's Fork River near Island Park, Idaho. And as I sit here now, in Ketchum, Idaho, I think about how my life has changed in the past ten years. I find that I think about the wind and the time of the day. I think about what bugs are hatching on which rivers all across the West. I think about the huge *Californica pteronarcys* hatch as well as the tiny *Callibaetis* flies that fill the air, making it sometimes difficult and dangerous to breathe. I wonder if Pale Moon Duns actually think about things. I wonder if fish have feelings and I marvel at their ability to survive in incredibly hostile waters. I think about the complexity of life and how interconnected all things are.

A fly rod in my hand feels like it should be there. It is an instrument I can control with ease. The lift of the line off the water and the movement of the line through air are a closely choreographed ballet. The rod is an extension of my body. The slight movements of my body while I cast my line are a romantic dance. The cast is graceful, full of feeling and gentleness. It's also the end result of tens of thousands of previous casts. It has not come easy. It has taken years to acquire and I have not yet perfected it. In time, I'll get better.

Fly-fishing is not about catching fish. It's about appreciating art and developing our own abilities.

It's about expanding our understanding of the world. It's about growth. It's about appreciating the beauty of all living things. It can be about putting meat in the freezer, but it's also about becoming a better person.

I think about how mercury from acid rain has spoiled the water and ruined the fish in so many lakes around the country. I think about Schroon Lake near my home in upstate New York; no one is allowed to eat more than one fish a month from the lake because of excessive mercury. Lake George, my home lake, will no doubt be next. (Pollution and the acid rain caused by it are a crime against all life. It should be remedied. To not do so is both criminal and cowardly.)

Many people who take up fly-fishing eventually give it up. This sport is not immediately gratifying. It takes time. It can also be very expensive. At best, it's very complicated. I can go for days and not catch anything. Regardless of how much we know, fish are unpredictable. Sometimes they strike and sometimes they don't. It's not personal.

And so I sit here in the darkness at the Old Faithful Inn. I listen to the quiet music still emanating from the speakers. I watch, momentarily, the caretaker as he polishes the ground floor and stores more wood in the box next to the massive fireplace. I personally thank him for his efforts to preserve this great hall.

During the next few weeks I'll probably fish with many different friends on the Gallatin and the Madison and the Fire Hole and other rivers as well. We may even drive over to the Smith River in California for a few early kings. I am forever thankful for the opportunities before me. I'll try to do my best. Sometimes life is good. I thank the spirits for being alive.

RESOURCES

The number-one thing to keep in mind when it comes to fishing is that you get what you pay for. I've had far better luck with quality stuff than with "el cheapo" gear bought just to save a few bucks. At the same time, I've been told many times to trust no one when it comes to fishing; guides just might try to fill their vacant dates by telling you the fish are biting and salesmen in fly shops might try to sell you a bunch of stuff that they've had sitting on their shelves for years. In truth, it's a tough call. The best advice is to know the rivers and to know what the fish are eating at any given time of the year. The old adage that "knowledge is power" is true under any circumstance.

Good fly rods are critical, as is good gear. But more important is your ability to use the equipment correctly. Beginners should absolutely, positively take a few casting lessons or attend a workshop designed by professionals for beginners. Even after throwing hundreds of thousands of casts, I still learn a few things whenever I fish with a competent guide.

Many organizations around the country offer lessons and workshops and also endorse lodges, fly shops and guides. It's definitely to your advantage to take your time with fly-fishing. It is not an immediate-gratification sport. Like learning to play a musical instrument, casting at its best is a skilled, finely tuned body movement that takes time to learn. So take a few lessons and don't get frustrated when your fly doesn't land exactly where you want it.

Many companies today make excellent fly rods in great variety. I've been fortunate to try out (and own) lots of different fly rods. Each has its own feel and each is made for different types of fish and fishing situations. Most of the professional rod companies offer guarantees on their gear. Although I have my favorites, within a few minutes of picking up a new rod I can adjust to its nuances. There are also tons of great reel manufacturers and companies who manufacture lines of all sorts, leaders, waders, nets and everything else imaginable.

The best advice I can offer is to fish with a professional guide who has good gear and will let you fish with different equipment. Although expensive gear never helped me catch a bigger fish, when you're hundreds of miles from nowhere in Alaska, you don't want you gear to fail.

To contact the author:
RalphKylloeGallery@ralphkylloe.com

FLY SHOPS, CATALOGS AND GEAR

BASS PRO SHOPS
www.basspro-shops.com

On-line shopping for everything the fiser-man needs, from gear to accessories, flies to apparel.

CABELA'S
800.237.4444
www.cabelas.com

For at-home or on the river, this on-line catalog offers an extensive collection of both medium- and high-priced quality gear. They have at least a dozen brands of rods and reels, plus fly-tying materials, apparel and accessories.

DAN BAILEY FLY SHOP
209 West Park Street
Livingston, MT 59047
800.356.4052
406.222.1673
www.dan-bailey.com

The quintessential fly shop in the Yellowstone River range of Montana, the guides here are all professionals and they sell high-quality gear through their store and extensive catalog. In business since 1938, they know the local waters better than anyone. Visit their online fly-fishing shop.

THE FLY SHOP
4140 Churn Creek Road
Redding, CA 96002
800.669.3474
info@theflyshop.com

Offers on-line catalog sales, trips, guides and more stuff than you can shake a fly rod at.

G. LOOMIS, INC.
1359 Downriver Drive
Woodland, WA 98674
800.456.6647
fax: 360.225.7169
www.gloomis.com

IFLYSHOP ONLINE
800.435.2755
www.iflyshop.com

JOHN JELINEK CUSTOM FLIES
1975 Valley Ranch Circle
Prescott, AZ 86303
928.771.9741

L. L. BEAN
800.441.5713
www.llbean.com

Complete shopping services on-line. plus locations of their retail stores and factory stores nationwide. Request their free Fly Fishing catalog.

NORTH FORK ANGLERS
1107 Sheridan Avenue
Cody, WY 82414
307.527.7274
www.northforkanglers.com

This fly shop offers high-quality gear and is located in the heart of some of the greatest fly-fishing areas of the country. Guide Andy Fisher will take you to some of the most gorgeous and productive (and uncrowded!) waters you'll ever see. And be sure to have breakfast at the Irma Hotel right across the street!

ON THE CREEK SEDONA OUTFITTERS
274 Apple Avenue, #C
Sedona, AZ 86336
928.203.9973

This is a full-service fly shop. The professional guides know the local waters and will give you a truthful assessment whether it's worth the time to go fishing. And right next door is a great Mexican restaurant!

THE ORVIS COMPANY
1711 Blue Hills Drive
Roanoke, VA 24012
888.235.9763
www.orvis.com

The Orvis company, arguably the largest and most visible of the fly fishing equipment companies, not only offers high-quality gear but also endorses guides and lodges throughout North America, as do their many retail stores throughout the country. They offer international trips to exotic places for great fishing. The Orvis catalogs are complete with more high-end stuff then you can shake a stick at and their outlet stores are Meccas where low-income fly fishermen (like myself) can get great deals on the latest gear. An endorsement by Orvis is an assurance of quality.

REDINGTON FLY ROD COMPANY
12715 Miller Road NE, #101
Bainbridge Island, WA 98110
800.253.2538
206.780.5465
www.redington.com

Builders of quality fly rods at affordable prices. They also offer high-quality apparel.

R. L. WINSTON ROD COMPANY
500 South Main Street
PO Box 411
Twin Bridges, MT 59754
406.684.5674
www.winstonrods.com

SAGE FLY RODS
Sage Manufacturing
8500 Northeast Day Road
Bainbridge Island, WA 98110
800.253.2538
206.842.6608
www.sageflyfish.com

SCOTT FLY ROD COMPANY
2355 Air Park Way
Montrose, CO 81401
800.728.7208
www.scottflyrod.com

ST. CROIX RODS
856 4th Avenue North
PO Box 279
Park Falls, WI 54552

800.826.7042
715.762.3226
www.stcroixrods.com

SUNRISE FLY SHOP
472 Main Street
Melrose, MT 59743
406.835.3474
www.sunriseflyshop.com

Servicing the Big Hole, Beaver Head and other rivers in the Melrose and Dillon, Montana, area. They offer great guides, including Chuck Paige, a local legend when it comes to fly-fishing. They have an excellent selection of gear. If you want great action, check this place out the second week of June during the salmon fly hatch.

WESTERN RIVERS FLY-FISHER
1071 E 900 S
Salt Lake City, UT 84105
800.545.4312
801.521.6424
www.wrflyfisher.com

Special thanks for generously lending the flies to photograph and use for the chapter openers throughout the book. Flies

include: Fat Albert, Prince Nymph, Red Fox Squirrel Nymph, Bullet Head Cricket, Green Butt Skunk, Bullet Head Cicada, Brown Drake, Rusty Bomber, Grey Ghost, Copper John, Green Butt Silver Hilton, Skwalla Stonefly, Chernobyl Ant, Elk Hair Caddis, Goddard's Caddis, Dave's Hopper, A. P. Emerger, Muddler Minnow, Blue Charm, Yellow Humpy, Zonker, Spruce Fly, Pheasant Tail, Parachute Brown Drake, Hornberg, Golden Stone Nymph, Ninja Cicada, Royal P. M. X., Foam Flying Ant, Spider and Henry's Fork Salmon Fly.

RODS AND REELS

ADIRONDACK SPORT SHOP
Fran Betters
PO Box 125
Wilmington, NY 12997
518.946.2605
www.adirondackflyfishing.com

Fran is a living legend in the fly-fishing world. He builds great rods and can offer great tips on how to catch fish in the Adirondacks.

BLACK BASS ANTIQUES
Henry Caldwell
PO Box 788
Bolton Landing, NY 12814
518.644.2389

Henry has a great shop in the Adirondacks full of antique fly-fishing gear.

BLUE HERON ANTIQUES
Hugh Chatham and Dan McClain
101 Main Street
PO Box 1309
Ennis, MT 59729
888.BLHERON

These folks have a great shop in the capital of fly-fishing in the northern Rockies where they also create custom fly rods. They authored Art of the Creel, *a must-have for all fly-fishing libraries.*

HEXAGRAPH FLY ROD COMPANY
2703 Rocky Woods
Kingwood, TX 77339
713.464.0505
fax: 713.464.5290
hexagraph@hexagraph.com

IRA STUTZMAN CUSTOM FLY RODS
Presented by Dan Fallon Hell's Canyon
Custom Rods
PO Box 733
Halfway, OR 97834
541.742.4828
www.fallonfly.com

Offers high-quality bamboo rods.

RYAN ASHLEY
3932 Bluebird Road
Kelowna, BC, Canada
V1W 1X6
250.764.4896

Builds high-quality rods from Sage blanks. His work is superb. I ought to know — I own four of his rods.

R. B. MEISLER FLY RODS
Ashland, OR
541.770.9522

Tough, durable and gorgeous rods are exceptionally well crafted and handle like a dream.

R. L. NUNLEY
2320 Central Street
Poteau, OK 74953
918.647.0496
www.caneman@clnk.com

Arguably the finest bamboo rod maker alive, his rods are sought-after treasures. With more than fifty years' experience in the rod-building business, his craftsmanship (and ability to catch great fish!) is evident.

SHENANDOAH RODS
Chris Bogart
490 Grandview Drive
Luray, VA 22835
540.743.7169

Chris builds high-end bamboo rods for discriminating fly fishermen.

STREAMSIDE CUSTOM FLY RODS
Kelly Newman
2085 N. Abbe
Fairview, MI 48621
989.848.5983

Kelly builds very high-end fly rods and also offers a professional guiding service in central Michigan.

YUKIHIRO YOSHIDA
2-25 Hatsuhi-cho, Mizuho-ku
Nagoya, Japan
phone/fax: 0528.33.1779
fwnb3805@mb.infoweb.ne.jp

Mr. Yoshida builds extraordinary bamboo fly rods, carrying on a centuries-old Japanese tradition.

Nothing is more humiliating than getting the fish of a lifetime on the end of your line and then losing it because your reel failed. This has happened to me and it's not fun. So I suggest that you purchase a high-quality reel put on high-quality backing and line (with, of course, correctly tied knots!). Here are a few of the real quality brand names that come to mind, in addition to the standards such as Able, Waterworks, Tibor, Galvan, Sage, Loomis, Ross, Orvis, L.L. Bean, Bauer, Hardy and Lamson. These reels are available at just about any good fly shop or online:

G. LOOMIS, INC.
1359 Downriver Drive
Woodland, WA 98674
800.456.6647
fax: 360.225.7169
www.gloomis.com

REDINGTON FLY ROD COMPANY
12715 Miller Road NE, #101
Bainbridge Island, WA 98110
800.253.2538
206.780.5465
www.redington.com

Builder of quality fly rods at affordable prices. The also offer high-quality apparel.

R. L. WINSTON FLY ROD COMPANY
500 South Main Street
PO Box 411
Twin Bridges, MT 59754
406.684.5674
www.winstonrods.com

SAGE FLY RODS
Sage Manufacturing
8500 Northeast Day Road
Bainbridge Island, WA 98110
800.533.3004
206.842.6608
www.sageflyfish.com

SCOTT FLY ROD COMPANY
2355 Air Park Way
Montrose, CO 81401
800.728.7208
www.scottflyrod.com

ST. CROIX RODS
856 4th Avenue North
PO Box 279
Park Falls, WI 54552
800.826.7042
715.762.3226
www.stcroixrods.com

FLY-FISHING SCHOOLS

There are numerous fly-fishing schools around the country. In truth, I've never been to one, but I've spoken with tons of people who have. If you want to get up and running fast, then a school is the way to go. Programs range from one week to one-day intensive lessons. Realistically, the more time you put into a program the better.

When inquiring about the schools, ask about the instructors. Are they certified fly-fishing instructors? Ask for references from those who have attended their classes before and make certain that you call them.

Here are a few schools from around the country that have solid reputations:

THE BLUE QUILL ANGLER FLY-FISHING SCHOOL
Evergreen, CO
800.435.5353
www.bluequillangler.com

The Blue Quill Angler offers numerous programs for those interested in learning the art of fly-fishing, including women's fishing groups, parent/child, beginning and advanced workshops. To make reservations through the Orvis Colorado Fly Fishing School, call 800.239.2074 extension 728.

CALIFORNIA SCHOOL OF FLY-FISHING
Nevada City, CA 95959
530.470.9005
www.flyline.com
cutter@flyline.com

Owned and operated by Ralph and Lisa Cutter, this is a serious professional school run by experienced fly-fishing instructors.

ORVIS FLY FISHING SCHOOLS
www.orvis.com
Located around the country. Find them on-line.

TROUT ON THE FLY
161 McCreedy Road
Chelsea, VT 05038
802.685.2100
www.troutonthefly.com

A great school for beginners as well as advanced fly fishermen. The service is excellent and you catch fish while you're learning.

WOMEN'S FLY-FISHING
PO Box 243963
Anchorage, AK 99524
www.womensflyfishing.net
pudge@womensflyfishing.net

A well-established school that teaches women to be competent fishermen. Not only do you learn in Alaska but you experience some of the greatest fishing the world has to offer.

LODGES

ALASKA TROPHY ADVENTURES
Charles Summerville
PO Box 474
Sylvan Beach, NY 13157
315.761.0941
www.alaskatrophyadventures.com
katmaifishing@aol.com

This outfit offers numerous extraordinary trips on the Alagnak River in the Katmai Forest of Alaska. They have some of the greatest salmon fishing in Icy Bay. I spent a week with them in 2003 and caught up to three hundred rainbows a day. They have comfortable, warm wooden cabins where great fishing is just a few steps outside your door. The meals are excellent and the guides are great. You'll fall in love with their three camp dogs that will entertain anyone for hours, as long as you're willing to throw sticks in the river! Further, they offer all kinds of trips across Alaska. This is a true wilderness experience where you'll see no other fisherman — just tens of thousands of salmon and trout.

THE ANGLER'S LODGE AT HENRY'S FORK
3431 Hwy 20
HC 66 Box 403
Last Chance, Island Park, ID 83429
208.558.9555
www.anglerslodge.net

This is a really great place on the Henry's Fork of the Snake River. Right outside their back door I landed both a 26-inch and a 24-inch rainbow before the sun was up!

BIG K RANCH
Highway 138 West
Elkton, OR 97436
800.390.BIGK
www.big-k.com

If you want someplace special, try the Big K in Oregon. The scenery is extraordinary, as are the lodge and meals. The

Umpqua River is the greatest smallmouth fishing I have ever experienced.

CHICO HOT SPRINGS LODGE
1 Chico Road
Pray, MT 59065
800.HOT.WADA
406.333.4933
www.chicohotsprings.com

This is one great place. Located just north of Yellowstone, you'll find that you spend just as much time in the extraordinary hot springs pool and eating at their restaurant as you do fishing the Yellowstone and other rivers in the immediate area.

CRYSTAL WOOD LODGE
38625 Westside Road
PO Box 1117
Klamath Falls, OR 97601
866.381.2322
www.crystalwoodlodge.com

Whether fishing ponds or streams, the fish are big in Crystal Creek near Klamath National Wildlife Refuge — really big! Be sure to have the prime rib or buffalo for dinner!

EAGLE ISLAND LODGE
PMB 335
35555 Spur Highway
Soldotna, AK 99669
877.262.9900
907.262.4050
www.eagleisland.net

A great small, rustic lodge on the shores of the lower Kenai, Eagle Island Lodge offers all kinds of regional Alaskan fishing trips and great accommodations.

GWIN'S LODGE
Bob Siter
14865 Sterling Highway
Cooper Landing, AK 99572
907.595.1266
www.gwinslodge.com

Historic Gwin's Lodge is the hub of all things fishing on the upper Kenai. Serving great meals and offering everything imaginable in their general store — from clothing to fishing gear to food and fish smoking and packaging services — this is the place to be for all species of

trout and salmon. They also offer great lodging at affordable prices.

HENDERSON SPRINGS
PO Box 220
Big Bend, CA 96011
888.337.0788
530.337.6917
www.hendersonsprings.com

Surrounded by impressive scenery fishermen have their choice of secluded lakes with huge trout or the nearby Pit River. Catch and release only on the lakes.

HUCKLEBERRY LODGE
1171 Big Pine Way
Forks, WA 98331
888.822.6008
360.374.6008
www.huckleberrylodge.com

Hidden away in the Hoh Rain Forest of Washington State is this small, personable lodge geared to the sportsman. If you walk away hungry from the breakfast table here, it's your own fault. This is one of the most scenic regions in the country. The moss-covered trees and the untouched Olympia Forest will give you goose bumps. The trout and steelhead fishing are great and all the guides are true professionals.

JAKE'S NUSHAGAK SALMON CAMP
PO Box 104179
Anchorage, AK 99510
907.522.1133
www.jakesalaska.com

Jake's, a tent camp in the wilds of Alaska, offers a variety of fishing experiences on the Nushagak and other Alaskan rivers. Clients are treated like family members as a significant number of fishermen return year after year, and the excellent meals are served family style. The guides are all pros, and if you can't catch the salmon of your dreams here, you might as well stay home. Enjoy the gorgeous scenery and watch for moose and waves of salmon while on the river.

KING PACIFIC LODGE
255 West 1st Street, Suite 214
North Vancouver, BC, Canada
V7M 3G8
888.592.5464
604.987.5452
www.kingpacificlodge.com

For five-star accommodations, incredible hospitality, stunning scenery, professionalism and absolutely great fishing, this is the place to go. The setting will take your breath away.

LEE'S FERRY LODGE
HC 67
PO Box 30
Marble Canyon, AZ 86036
800.962.9755
928.355.2261
www.leesferry.com

In the middle of nowhere, Lee's Ferry Lodge is a beacon in the night. The restaurant offers five-star meals, the rooms are clean and comfortable and the views are out of this world. This is a down-home kind of place with all the atmosphere of the Grand Canyon, rattlesnakes, cowboys and extraordinary fly-fishing.

LONESOME DUCK
32955 Hwy 97 North
Chiloquin, OR 97624
800.367.2540
steveh@lonesomeduck.com

Secluded and with big trout right out your front door, this is a very relaxed place with some of the greatest fishing in the West.

ONE HUNDRED ACRE WOOD B&B RESORT AND OUTDOOR ADVENTURE TOURS
PO Box 202
North Fork, ID 83466
208.865.2165
www.iloveinns.com

This is a great B&B located just a few miles down the road from Idaho's famous Salmon River. It's a charming place that offers great meals and great atmosphere. They also have an excellent trout pond in their backyard.

ORCA ADVENTURE LODGE
PO Box 2105
Cordova, AK 99574
1.866.424.ORCA
www.orcaadventurelodge.com

The Orca Adventure Lodge is a full-service facility located in the quaint town of Cordova, Alaska. The lodge is located in a historic salmon-canning factory, where just out the front door you'll find killer whales, otters by the dozens and salmon. They also offer numerous fly-in trips to remote camps along the Lost Coast. This is a great place. Their out-camp on the Katalla River is the best silver salmon fishery I've ever seen. If you can't catch fifty huge, dancing silvers a day here on a fly rod, you're not trying. This is one place where you won't find crowds, but watch out for bears and huge silvers because by the middle of the day you'll be exhausted.

PAPOOSE CREEK LODGE
1520 Highway 287 North
Cameron, MT 59720
888.674.3030
www.papoosecreek.com

Situated in the Yellowstone eco-region, this world-class lodge is only minutes away from world-class trout fishing on the Madison River.

RIVERSIDE LODGE BED AND BREAKFAST
6150 Ferguson Road
Port Alberni, BC, Canada
V9Y 7L5
250.723.3474
www.canadianbedbreakfast.com

This lodge is a high-end log cabin B&B located on the shores of the famous Stamp River on Vancouver Island. Just out your backdoor you can catch all the salmon and steelhead you want. It's my favorite place on the island!

RIZUTO'S SAN JUAN RIVER LODGE
PO Box 6309
1796 HWY 173
Navajo Dam, NM 87419
www.rizutos.net

Known as one of the best trout streams in America, the San Juan River offers technical challenges and fish like none other in the region. The lodge is a casual setting with comfortable clean rooms.

SEVEN LAKES LODGE
PO Box 39
Edwards, CO 81632
800.809.4772
970.926.7813
www.sevenlakeslodge.com

Seven Lakes is a big-ticket place offering gourmet food, exceptional rooms, great service and world-class fishing — all in a gorgeous area.

SORENSEN'S RESORT
14255 HWY 88
Hope Valley, CA 96120
800.423.9949

This is a cozy facility with thirty cabins and a main lodge whose setting is the Carson River, offering great fishing and great activities.

THE STEAMBOAT INN
42705 N. Umpqua Hwy.
Steamboat, OR 97447
800.840.8825
www.thesteamboatinn.com

A very cozy retreat with breathtaking views of the Umpqua. This is a rugged area that will delight anyone in the least bit interested in fly-fishing. Loved by Zane Grey, the Umpqua River offers an impressive run of steelhead as well as great scenery.

TETON VALLEY LODGE
379 Adams Rd
Driggs, ID 83422
208.354.8124
800.455.1182
Winter
208.354.2386
800.455.1182
www.tetonvalleylodge.com
info@tetonvalleylodge.com

Teton Valley Lodge has been in operation since 1919. They offer great fishing on numerous waters in the Teton range and specialize in fishing with dry flies.

GUIDES

AMBASSADOR GUIDES SERVICES INC.
PO Box 6229
Marble Canyon, AZ 86036
800.256.7596
www.ambassadorguides.com

If you get the chance to fish Lee's Ferry, you have to fish with Bill McBurney of Ambassador Guide Services. Incredibly accommodating, he's as professional as they come and knows the local waters and the ecology. He's also a great teacher. He taught my four-year-old daughter to fly-fish and she landed her first trout on the Colorado!

BILL VON BRUNDEL
3474 Hammond Bay Road
Nanaimo, BC, Canada
V9T 1E6
1.877.3FISHON
justfishn@islandnet.com

Bill is one of those obsessive individuals who pursues fish relentlessly. An expert caster and fly-tier, he'll walk for miles through rugged terrain just to put his clients on fish. He knows the rivers of the island like the back of his hand. When the steelhead and silver salmon are in, he'll be there to greet them.

ED LINK
North Fork, ID
800.259.6866

Ed Link is the "old man" on the Salmon River in Idaho. Respected by everyone who knows him, his experience on the river is profound. Adept at catching salmon and steelhead, even the most seasoned pros can learn something from him. He's also the only guide to ever grill me a bacon-wrapped filet mignon for lunch in his guide boat.

JOEY IRONS
PO Box 911
Ennis, MT 59729
406.682.5040
406.539.2211
joeirons@3rivers.net
Joey fishes the great rivers of southwestern Montana. I've fished with him many times on the Madison and other rivers in that region. He's a professional guide who will tell you beforehand if the fish are biting or not and can help you catch a huge brown or rainbow in just about any season. He's also one of the few guides who can make a great photograph!

KEITH SHORTS
630 Cache Creek Drive
Jackson, WY 83001
307.733.8495

I've fished with Keith many times over the years. His ability to teach beginners and experienced fly fishermen new things is keen. He knows the hidden places in the Jackson Hole area and successfully fishes many of the rivers in the northern Rocky Mountains.

MILLER'S RIVERBOAT SERVICE
Luke Conner
PO Box 940127
Houston, AK 99694
907.892.6872
907.841.4860

Luke Conner is one of the best young guides in Alaska. I've fished with him for years and caught more fish than I can remember. He's fished all over Alaska and is presently fishing the Willow and Talkeetna areas for huge rainbows and salmon.

MYSTIC WATERS FLY-FISHING
Fred Telleen
PO Box 791
Cooper Landing, AK 99572
907.227.0549
www.mysticfishing.com

Fred, perhaps one of the greatest guides in all of North America, offers trips on the famous Kenai River in Alaska. He uses high-quality gear for his clients, pays meticulous attention to every detail and can get you a fish when no one else can!

PAT GRAHAM
121 Coho Drive
Forks, WA 98331
360.374.5313
360.640.0956
www.fishingnorthwest.com

A seasoned pro, Pat fishes the mysterious waters of the Hoh Rain Forest in Washington State. A lifelong guide, his intimate knowledge of the waters and the fish will help any client catch the fish of a lifetime.

THE RIVER'S EDGE
Mike Blanck
2012 North 7th Avenue
Bozeman, MT 59715
406.586.5373
www.theriversedge.com

The River's Edge offers complete guiding services on local waters. They are also a professional fly shop with sales people who know what they are talking about.

SILVER CLOUD EXPEDITIONS
Chris Swersey and Mary Wright
PO Box 1006
Salmon, ID 83467
877.756.6215
www.silvercloudexp.com

Silver Cloud offers a full range of fishing and camping adventures on the extraordinary Salmon River in Idaho, a river you should fish at least once in your lifetime.

SILVER CREEK OUTFITTERS
500 North Main Street
Ketchum, ID 83340
800.732.5687
208.726.5282
www.silver-creek.com

In the Ketchum area, Silver Creek Outfitters is the place to go for gear, clothing, lessons and guides. Offering a full range of experiences on local rivers, their guides are knowledgeable professionals capable of teaching beginners as well as providing unforgettable experiences for advanced fly fishermen.

WILD TROUT FLY-FISHING OUTFITTERS
J. D. Bingman
PO Box 160003
Big Sky, MT 59716
406.995.4895
406.995.2975

A great fly shop on the shores of the Gallatin River that offers a professional guide service on the local waters of the Yellowstone ecosystem.

WORLDCAST ANGLERS, LTD.
PO Box 766
Wilson, WY 83014
800.654.0676
gofish@worldcastanglers.com

Offering a full range of fly-fishing services in the Wyoming region, this group of professionals provides trips in the Rocky Mountains and on international waters.

SHOWS AND MAGAZINES

One other fishing venue should not be overlooked. Certainly the greatest place to see and try all the equipment ever conceived and produced by the human race is at fly-fishing and sportsman's shows. I've been to many of these around the country, and when I've attended with non-fly fishermen I've had to be dragged out. These events are great conventions where everyone has an opinion and new products to sell. You'll also find tons of guides and lodges exhibiting and there is almost always a place to cast the latest fly rods and reels.

The best way to find these shows is to search the Internet (type in FLY FISHING SHOWS on any search engine), or watch your local newspapers for places and dates. Or subscribe to *Wild On The Fly* magazine, which offers a three-month posting for all the shows in the country. Denver, Los Angles, Danbury, Ct., College Park, Charleston, and many other cities host such shows. When you go, just give yourself plenty of time and don't go with non-fishermen!